Tom Ferris

THE IRISH

NARROW GAUGE

A Pictorial History

Volume One
From Cork to Cavan

**On 15th September 1929 the first two
engines supplied to the Cork & Muskerry
Light Railway await their next turn of duty
outside the running shed at the railway's
Cork Western Road terminus.**
H.C.Casserley.

For Catherine

© 1993
Tom Ferris

Published by
The Blackstaff Press Limited
3 Galway Park, Dundonald
Belfast, BT16 0AN
Northern Ireland

ISBN 0-85640-517-5

Printed and bound by
Woolnough Bookbinding Limited
Irthlingborough, Northants.
NN9 5SE

Designed by
Midland Publishing
and Stephen Thompson Associates.

Typeset in
Garamond and Gill Sans

Front cover photograph:
**On the 1st July 1938, as the 1.45pm
train from Schull to Skibbereen pauses at
Holyhill, it is overtaken by a more
traditional form of transport.**
H.C.Casserley.

Title page photograph:
**At Drumshambo on the Cavan & Leitrim
section of CIE, the former Tralee & Dingle
2-6-0T No.3, prepares to leave with a train
for Arigna. This picture was taken in March
1959, and the line had only another four
weeks left before closure.**
H.C.Casserley.

Tom Ferris

THE IRISH

NARROW GAUGE

A Pictorial History

Volume One
From Cork to Cavan

THE
BLACKSTAFF
PRESS

BELFAST

PREFACE AND ACKNOWLEDGEMENTS

THE REASONS that led me to write this book and its sequel are outlined in the introduction, but the catalyst which turned my interest in the Irish narrow gauge into a determination to write about it, was a telephone conversation with my old friend Fergal Tobin in Dublin. For the purposes of our Irish railway publishing projects he fills the role of the apocryphal man in the Clapham, or in this case more appropriately, the Clontarf, omnibus. His positive reaction played a significant part in translating an idea into a reality and encouraged me to proceed with the research.

As soon as I began work on the project, the usual suspects were rounded up and thanks are once again due to Clifton Flewitt, Des McGlynn, and Derek Young. The number of people who actively assisted me at various stages in the research, both in Britain and Ireland, makes such a long list that I sincerely hope that I have not left anyone out, and if I have, I hope they will contact me so that the omission may be corrected in a future edition.

For this first volume I was most fortunate in being able to enlist the help of the acknowledged expert on the narrow gauge in Munster, Walter McGrath. His assistance was also of inestimable value on the appendix dealing with the narrow gauge in industry and his generosity in allowing me access to the photographic collection which he has built up over many years and his willingness to respond to my many queries and questions, must also be acknowledged. Further information and photographs on the Cork lines were kindly supplied by Dermot McCarthy.

Many individuals and organisations have provided the photographs which grace these pages. Photographers who have provided pictures for this first volume have included Desmond Coakham, John Edgington, J.H.Price and W.A.C.Smith. Richard Casserley has allowed me to use many of his late father's superb pictures of the Irish narrow gauge covering a period from the 1920s onwards. Len's of Sutton must be thanked for the loan of a large collection of Irish negatives and Graham Stacey of the Locomotive Club of Great Britain could not have been more helpful in allowing me to publish material from the Ken Nunn collection which is in the custodianship of the Club. Peter Kelly and Chris Milner, the editor and assistant editor of the *Railway Magazine* – in my view still the best general interest railway periodical on the market, were kind enough to allow me access to some of their copious files and to publish some of the pictures therein. Some splendid early pictures came from the collection of W.H.Butler. Other pictures came from Norman Johnson and Richard Whitford. Thanks are due to Liam Queally and Joseph Sloan for their help in various ways and I must not forget Tim Shuttleworth for his skills as a photographic printer of the highest order. His ability to project negatives (including the occasional sow's ear), into silk-purse-like prints, was combined with an ability to meet the very tight turn round times I kept having to ask him for. I cheerfully commend his work to one and all.

The book has been greatly enhanced in my view, through the use of extracts from the 1 inch series of Ordnance Survey maps produced before the First World War. Permission to reproduce these has been kindly granted by the Irish Ordnance Survey in Dublin. I would like to thank the staff of the Survey Office for their courtesy and for the speed with which they dealt with our requests for copies of the maps in question, at a time when they were inundated with other work.

Once again I am indebted to my colleague Chris Salter of Midland Publishing for his tireless work in steering the book through the production process. We were also fortunate in being able to work with Stephen Thompson, not just because of his skill as a designer, but because he combines this with a passion for railways which has made this book for him, a labour of love.

In compiling a photographic record of the Irish narrow gauge I set myself certain parameters. With the exception of the industrial lines, the railways represented had to be in effect, common carriers, thus urban tramways have been excluded. This has led me to leave out the Dublin and Lucan Tramway, on the grounds that I see it as an adjunct to Dublin's urban transportation network, rather than a significant narrow gauge line in its own right.

In the case of each system I have tried to give a succinct history of the concern.

The photographic section provides coverage of the line's loco fleet, attempts a pictorial journey along its length and where possible includes some pictures of specific items of rolling stock in the hope that these may encourage railway modellers to tackle the wealth of opportunities which the Irish narrow gauge has to offer.

As the century has worn on, photography has generally become easier and more accessible. The picture selection tends to be loaded towards the 1950s for those lines which survived that long simply because there were more pictures of higher quality to choose from as time went on. I have also tried to use unpublished pictures, though in many cases this proved impossible.

Over many decades photographers and collectors of photographs have recorded and preserved a great deal of material on the Irish narrow gauge. It has been my deliberate intention to seek out such sources rather than rake through the well known and much used national collections yet again.

I have seen my role as the publisher, in the truest sense of the word, that of bringing to the attention of the public, all the work done by these individual photographers, well known and anonymous, and that of those who have conserved their material over the years.

What follows in these pages is not just railway history but a slice of social and economic history, a memorial to an era now firmly embedded in the past and a tribute to those who took the trouble to preserve it in pictorial form for future generations.

Tom Ferris
Shrewsbury, May 1993

CONTENTS

INTRODUCTION

URING the course of writing my first book *Irish Railways in Colour: From Steam to Diesel 1955-1967,* (Midland Publishing, 1992), I became more and more absorbed in the narrow gauge railways of Ireland. That Ireland had a substantial network of 3ft gauge lines was something that I had always taken for granted without giving very much thought as to why they came to be there in the first place. My exploration of the three systems that survived into the 1950s for that first book, got me thinking more and more about the very diverse lines that made up the Irish narrow gauge. The consummation of that train of thought and the search for answers to some of the questions it raised have led to these books.

I started out with the limited perspective of someone interested in these railways simply as railways which had quaint or unusual locos and rolling stock or offered a fairly erratic service through some of the most picturesque yet remote parts of Ireland. I finished up with the realisation that these lines had to be considered in the context of the economic, social and even political circumstances that led to their construction, for many of them to make any sense whatsoever. Whilst this is important and I have tried to bear it in mind and reflect it in the course of the books, I cannot deny that the other great attraction of the Irish narrow gauge was the sheer diversity of the various lines and the total lack of standardisation or uniformity which they exuberantly manifested.

My original intention was to cover the Irish narrow gauge in one book but as the research progressed and more and more interesting pictures turned up the manuscript grew in size to such an extent that the book was either going to be prohibitively expensive or would have to suffer drastic cuts. Faced with these unpalatable options we decided to publish the work in two volumes. This book deals with the 3ft gauge railways in the southern part of Ireland starting with the lines in County Cork and moving northwards to conclude with the Cavan & Leitrim Railway. Volume two covers the lines located in the province of Ulster. Whilst County Cavan is of course in that province, I hope readers will excuse

this intentional geographical solecism, made on the grounds of the need to have both volumes of roughly equal size and also because only the most northerly 12 miles or so of the C&L strayed into Ulster. By publishing the work in this format those readers whose interest lie with a particular system will find that line covered in a more comprehensive manner than might have been possible otherwise had we tried to squeeze the whole of Ireland's extensive narrow gauge systems into one volume. All the lines in this first volume, with the exception of the Lartigue monorail in County Kerry which closed in 1924, became part of the Great Southern Railway on its formation in 1925. The GSR only absorbed these lines which were wholly located within the Irish Free State. The two big narrow gauge systems in County Donegal, the Londonderry & Lough Swilly and the County Donegal Railways, escaped the clutches of the GSR because short sections of their lines entered the territory of Northern Ireland. In one of those paradoxes, found so often in Ireland, County Donegal, in geographical terms Ireland's most northerly county, is politically speaking, in 'the south', meaning that it is part of the Irish Republic. These quirks of Irish geo-politics have helped us in deciding the dividing line between the two volumes. This book concerns itself with the GSR lines, the second volume deals with the others.

Though each volume is complete in itself this is, in effect, the introduction to both books. I have tried to look at the narrow gauge railways of Ireland as an entity and draw out the features they had in common. It would be dangerous to try and expound a great all embracing theory to explain the growth of the narrow gauge, however I believe that certain threads can be traced, which though never strong enough to bind these lines together into a coherent network or an alternative to the broad gauge, do help to explain the spread of the 3ft gauge from the 1870s onwards. The reasons that led to the development of the narrow gauge in the first place also contained the seeds of its downfall in the changed circumstances of the twentieth century which the nineteenth century narrow gauge promoters could never have foreseen.

At its peak around the time of the Great War, there were 537 route miles of 3ft gauge track open for public service in Ireland. There was a far greater concentration of narrow gauge lines in Ireland than in the rest of the United Kingdom. The nature of these Irish lines was also different from those in Scotland, England and Wales. With the exception of the Campbeltown & Machrihanish and the Glasgow Underground, the narrow gauge was almost unknown in Scotland. The well known and still largely extant narrow gauge lines of north Wales had been built, in the main to cater for the needs of the slate industry. The English narrow gauge lines can be divided into those built for a particular industrial purpose, like the Snailbeach Railway in Shropshire, or to service a military establishment such as the lines at Chatham Dockyard, or to open up a specific resort or tourist attraction. I cheerfully acknowledge that the foregoing is both a generalisation and an over simplification and does not present the full picture of the narrow gauge in Britain. It does however serve to illustrate the point that I wish to make which is that, with a few minor exceptions, the Irish narrow gauge lines were all common carriers, which offered all the services, both passenger and goods, that would have been expected of any standard gauge railway. It is this and the extent of the narrow gauge in Ireland that marks out the Irish lines as being different.

The concept of narrow gauge railways was almost as old as the beginnings of the ascendancy of the Stephensons' 4ft 8½in as the standard gauge that was to dominate the railways of the world. One of the questions which I set out to answer in the course of my research, and which I have to admit I have failed to explain to my satisfaction, was, why did the 3ft gauge come to be adopted as Ireland's narrow gauge? The Festiniog Railway in Wales opened in 1836 on a gauge of 1ft 11in and was followed by other sub-standard gauge lines over the next few decades. In the far flung reaches of the British Empire there was a growing application of narrower gauges in the 1860s. The first railway in New Zealand, a mineral line, was laid to a gauge of 3ft. In Australia, Queensland opened its first 3ft

6in gauge line in 1865 and back in Wales the Festiniog pioneered the use of steam traction on the narrow gauge from 1863 onwards. Charles Spooner of the Festiniog Railway was an enthusiastic advocate of the narrow gauge and whilst there is no direct evidence linking him to any of the early Irish narrow gauge lines there is some circumstantial evidence that forms a connection from the Festiniog Railway to Ireland via the Isle of Man.

The first time the narrow gauge was authorised for an Irish railway that was actually built, was in July 1872, when the Act of Parliament granted to the Ballymena, Cushendall & Red Bay Railway specifically allowed the Company to build its line to a gauge of between 2 and 3ft. In the same year the private mineral line of the Glenariff Iron Ore & Harbour Company began operations. This railway, running on private land and thus not requiring an Act of Parliament, was built to the 3ft gauge. Both of these lines in Antrim were activated just after the 3ft gauge had been adopted by the Isle of Man Railway Company which had been launched at the end of 1870. The IMR engineer Henry Vignoles, is known to have had contact with the Festiniog Railway and it is reasonable to trace his recommendation of the 3ft gauge to his observations in Wales. Given the geographical proximity of the Isle of Man to the north of Ireland and the links provided by coastal shipping between the two areas, I find it inconceivable that the gauge adopted by the GIO&H and the BC&RB was not influenced by events in the Isle of Man. Further circumstantial evidence may be found in the fact that two of the first three locomotives supplied to another Antrim narrow gauge line, the Ballymena & Larne, which began operations in 1877, were very similar to those built by Beyer Peacock for the Isle of Man Railway. Of course once the 3ft gauge was established and seen to be effective in County Antrim, it was logical for other Irish lines to adopt it and thus it became, in effect, Ireland's second standard gauge.

The overriding reason why railway promoters felt the need to depart from a national standard gauge is that of cost. Any break of gauge presents its own problems. Tran shipment of goods and passengers from one gauge to another is both time con-

suming and costly and there have to be pressing economic arguments for this to be contemplated. In the case of Ireland to appreciate the reasons for the popularity of the narrow gauge at the end of the nineteenth century, it is necessary to look at the economic history of the country in the years since the 1840s.

In 1841 the population of Ireland was over eight million. If normal demographic trends had been followed it should have been over nine million by 1851. In fact in that year it had fallen to 6½ million because of the effects of the Famine which began in 1845 and ran through until 1849. A substantial proportion of Ireland's population was

A number of the Irish narrow gauge lines ran, for all or part of the way, alongside the public road. This feature, not uncommon on the continent, was rare in the British Isles outside Ireland. Here ex Tralee & Dingle 2-6-0T No.3 heads along the Arigna section of the Cavan & Leitrim line with a mixed train in May 1957. D.G.Coakham.

dependent for subsistence on the potato and the failure of that crop in successive years through the spread of blight, traumatised the country. To deaths through malnutrition and disease was added the diaspora of emigration, all of which caused the immediate drop in the population. This decline continued into the second half of the twentieth century when at last the trend was arrested and the population of Ireland began to stabilise and, only in recent years, to expand slowly.

The failure of the British government at first to appreciate the seriousness of the sit-

uation and later, to act to alleviate the effects of the Famine, provoked a legacy of lasting bitterness in Ireland but also ensured that in the future the established economic ethos of *laissez-faire* would be rethought as far as Ireland was concerned at least. Ireland began to be treated differently from the rest of the kingdom. Parts of the country were desperately poor and if the disaster of the Famine was not to be repeated, official attitudes towards Ireland would have to change. This has an important bearing on our story.

Adam Smith, that great eighteenth century prophet of free market economics, was not opposed to the state becoming involved in improvements to what we would now call infrastructure. Were he alive today, he would probably give his blessing to a decent railway linking London and the Channel Tunnel. In Ireland, since the eighteenth century, government commissioners had been active in promoting improvements to waterways, fisheries and the draining of bog land. In the 1830s, faced with the chaos of competing gauges in Britain, the government set up the Drummond Commission, to establish a standard gauge for the railways of Ireland, before construction there got under way. The Irish Board of Works, reconstituted in 1831, was active from the 1850s onwards in arbitrating in disputes between railway companies and landowners and from the 1870s in providing loans to assist railway construction. The most spectacular government interventions in the late nineteenth century were in the realms of the ownership of land. A series of Land Acts, financed by the state from the 1870s onwards, transformed the Irish peasantry from tenants into peasant proprietors in a generation.

This interventionist approach to Irish economic affairs was typified by the establishment in 1891 of the Congested Districts Board. This was set up to address the problems of the areas of acute poverty which ran from Donegal and Leitrim in the north, down the whole west of Ireland, to Cork and Kerry in the south. The term congested was rather a misnomer in that the population density of these areas was less than the national average. The districts so defined covered about 1/6th of the land area and 1/9th of the population of Ireland. The

Congested Districts Board instigated a wide variety of initiatives to improve the conditions of these areas. Whilst ultimately its main function became that of purchasing and redistributing land, dealing with over two million acres by 1923, it was active in developing agriculture and fisheries and improving roads and encouraging the construction of railways in the districts under its aegis. Such state sponsored economic activity is far removed from the normal picture of the *laissez-faire* attitude of the state to economic policy that we have of Victorian Britain. It is not surprising that this interventionist approach made itself felt in the field of railway promotion as well.

In the nineteenth century the railway appeared, to communities all over the British Isles, as the mark of civilisation. These were the arteries along which progress and prosperity flowed. It is not surprising that virtually every place of any substance, and indeed many places of virtually no substance, wanted one. Nor is it surprising, in the light of government attitudes towards Ireland, in the decades after the Famine, that support for railway promotion should play a part in official policy. Thus was the Irish railway system encouraged in a way that was unique in the British Isles. In the rest of the kingdom railway promotion was left largely to private companies and market forces and was defined by the profit motive and not at all by economic altruism. Whilst the main trunk lines of the Irish system were built in the traditional nineteenth century entrepreneurial fashion, to extend the system into the poorer and more remote regions where it was felt that railways had a vital role to play in the economic development of these areas, government policy played an active role in assisting the process. This should be seen in turn in the context of a broader economic policy which was to avoid at all costs a repetition of the disaster of the Famine.

From 1860 until the end of the century a series of Acts were passed to encourage the development of railways in Ireland. The first significant piece of legislation was the Tramways Act of 1883, which will crop up at regular intervals throughout the book. A number of 3ft gauge lines had been promoted before this Act, notably the three lines in County Antrim and the West Donegal. These companies had obtained parliamentary approval in the time honoured fashion and gone about raising their capital on the commercial markets in the normal way. The Tramways Act attempted to provide a stimulus to railway construction in potentially unremunerative areas by allowing railway promoters to approach a county's Grand Jury to seek financial support for their scheme.

The Grand Juries had been established in the seventeenth century as the administrative unit in each county. The members of the Grand Juries were in the main landowners and their principal function was to levy local taxation in the form of the county cess. Under the 1883 Act, if a scheme met the approval of the Grand Jury, that body could in turn, require the areas that were to benefit from the railway, to guarantee the interest on all or part of the capital required for the project. Each county was divided into districts or baronies hence the origin of the expression which we will frequently encounter, the baronial guarantee. The Tramways Act did not create the baronial guarantee but it did allow them to be applied to railway construction and in addition the Act allowed the Treasury, under certain strict conditions, to contribute to the costs of the guarantees. At first the baronial guarantees were restricted to narrow gauge lines and though this was later rescinded, it was a powerful incentive towards the spread of the 3ft gauge.

Interest on capital was guaranteed at 5%. This was more than many conventionally funded railways could often pay in dividends to their shareholders. Investment in railways in parts of Ireland which might be remote and under developed, if they had a baronial guarantee, was thus transformed for both private investors and finance houses, from being a venture of the greatest risk, into a meal ticket. Yet even with the guarantees it was sometimes difficult to raise the capital locally and the shares had to be placed with finance houses in London.

In some cases the Tramways Act encouraged promoters who knew little or nothing about railways to produce a line which was badly constructed and poorly managed. In addition, because the Grand Juries were undemocratic and represented the last official bastions of power of the discredited landlord class, there was always the possibility that the whim of the gentry to have a railway, could be satisfied only at the expense of the unfortunate ratepayers who would have to pick up the bill, and yet had no control over the dispensation of the guarantees in the first place. The friction that this could cause was apparent in the affairs of both the Tralee & Dingle and the Cavan & Leitrim at the end of the nineteenth century. Despite these potential failings, the Tramways Act was well intentioned and did lead to a significant expansion of the 3ft gauge.

In 1889 the Light Railways (Ireland) Act made state finance much more overt, containing provisions for government funding for lines which the Lord Lieutenant deemed to be in the public interest. This Act actually led to more broad than narrow gauge lines being constructed. The final significant piece of railway legislation was the Railways (Ireland) Act of 1896. This allowed the Treasury to provide grants from public funds to build railways where they were thought to be needed. The two lines which were built as a result of this Act, the Buncrana to Carndonagh and the Letterkenny to Burtonport extensions of the Londonery & Lough Swilly Railway, were clearly railways which would never have been built without massive handouts from the public purse. This generous public funding of private railways was not extended to the rest of the United Kingdom and has to be put in a political context.

In the 1880s and 1890s a consensus seemed to grow within the British establishment that Ireland's problems were fundamentally of an economic rather than a political nature. If the questions of land ownership could be resolved and Ireland was brought up to the levels of prosperity enjoyed by the rest of the kingdom, then the agitation for self government, which had bedevilled Westminster politics from the 1880s onwards, would die away. Whilst no policy document was ever written crystalizing this into a legislative programme, the signs of it are clear enough for some histories to refer to it as constructive unionism. Those of a more cynical disposition have described it as an attempt to kill home rule with kindness. In so far as this concerns our story, it is fair to say that very few of Ireland's narrow gauge lines would have been built if left to market forces alone. For those who disapprove of such government interference, the rapid decline of these lines in the twentieth century is evidence that projects such as these were bound to end in economic tears.

The narrow gauge was used in every instance on the grounds of cost, it being generally cheaper to construct narrow gauge lines than those built to the standard gauge. Once the line was built the economic advantages of the narrow gauge began to diminish. Whilst there were some savings in running costs it required much the same number of men to run trains on both systems. The extra costs imposed by the need to tran-ship goods could be considerable. If ever you have a bad day at work, think of the men who had to shovel Arigna coal by hand, from narrow to broad gauge wagons at Belturbet and Dromod, and I'll wager that your job will not seem that bad after all. The isolated independent narrow gauge lines had to have workshops equipped to do heavy repairs and some of them had stations far too grand for the business that they were likely to attract. The savings apparent to the promoters who plumped for the narrow gauge turned out to be illusory. Even in the years before the First World War, which are often perceived as the golden age of the railways, many of the 3ft gauge lines barely covered their operating costs from the revenue they generated, let alone earned enough to pay the guaranteed dividends on their capital. The ratepayers were called upon again and again to make up the difference. This was at a time when the railways had a virtual monopoly of any traffic that was going. It is easy to see how terribly vulnerable to road competition they were to be in the 1920s and '30s.

Did the money poured into the narrow gauge in the remoter parts of Ireland have any lasting effect in developing the country and bringing prosperity? The answer to this question is far from clear. Every group of promoters naturally emphasised the importance of their scheme in opening up the country it passed through and the benefits it would bring through its encouragement of trade and commerce. But this was a double edged sword. The railway might well make it easier for the produce of an area to be shipped out, but they also made the import of goods from outside a lot easier. It can be plausibly argued that the spread of railways in Ireland was in fact a cause of industrial decline. In 1841, according to the census of that year, 989,000 people were engaged in manufacturing. By 1881 this number had fallen to 379,000. Even allowing for the distortions caused by the Famine, this was a significant decline. Mills, distilleries, breweries and tanneries, and workshops for the manufacture of agricultural equipment were once commonplace in rural Ireland. The development of the railways meant that British imports could penetrate into the remotest corners of the island making local industries vulnerable to the cheaper and probably better products of the greatest manufacturing economy in the world. What is certainly true is that the Irish economy was more squarely based on agriculture at the end of the nineteenth century than it had been at the beginning.

What the railways did do was to facilitate the movement of people. To hundreds of thousands emigration seemed the only solution. For many emigrants the last tearful, receding view of their childhood home must have been framed by the window of a narrow gauge carriage in Cork, Clare and Kerry, or in the hills of Donegal. As late as 1890 it was recorded that a station master on the Cavan & Leitrim absconded with £8 in takings, this sum just happened to be the cost of a passage to the USA at the time.

We have noted the financial vulnerability of many of the narrow gauge lines in the years before the Great War. In the years after the war, lorries and buses became increasingly common sights in Ireland. As road vehicles increased in numbers, the road system was gradually improved to cope with them and narrow gauge lines began to close. If you share my view that a monorail

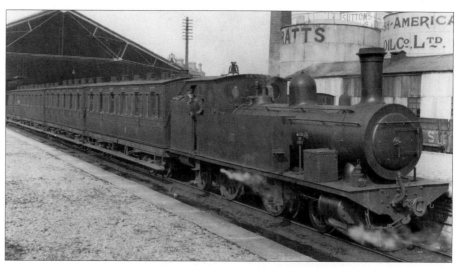

has the narrowest gauge of all, then the first to succumb was the uniquely bizarre Listowel & Ballybunion, in 1924. The Ballycastle Railway almost became the first conventional 3ft gauge line to go under, only to be rescued by the London, Midland & Scottish Railway / Northern Counties Committee in the same year that saw the demise of the L&B. The first 3ft gauge line to close was the Portstewart Tramway in 1926, when buses took over the service.

The contraction of the system gathered pace in the 1930s. The war had been responsible for major increases in costs. The price of coal had escalated as had wages, and the introduction of the eight hour day, whilst no one could deny its beneficial social effects, added proportionally higher costs to the railways. In this changed world most of the narrow gauge lines carried on as before – steam operated and labour intensive. By the 1920s and '30s, track, structures and rolling stock were also beginning to show their age and there was little or no money for renewals. Pre-war, a virtual monopoly of local traffic had just about seen the lines through, post-war increasing costs and falling traffic levels were quickly reflected in the balance sheets. With the notable exception of the County Donegal Railway, there was a general lack of technical innovation to try to meet the new circumstances in which the railways found themselves.

The lines most vulnerable were those left to their own devices in the 1920s. The takeover by the GSR of narrow gauge lines in the south saved most of them until the 1950s with the exception of the two which operated out of Cork City. The Antrim lines were at first secure in the bosom of the LMS and the CDR benefited from being jointly owned by the Great Northern Railway and the LMS. The first major system to get into difficulties was the Lough Swilly which had to struggle on independently without a more powerful protector. Because it ran

into Northern Ireland the GSR did not consider taking it over. The L&LSR is also the one line, which in my view suffered badly from the partition of Ireland, the border cutting off Derry from its natural hinterland in Donegal.

The great joy of the Irish narrow gauge was its sheer diversity. Each line was different from the others and had a character all of its own. Over fifty different classes of locomotives were put in service on the 3ft gauge and no class ever reached double figures in terms of numbers built. Standardisation was unheard of and the types of locos used ranged from 0-4-0 tram engines to the mighty 4-8-0 tender engines of the L&LSR. Though some lines were notable pioneers of electric and diesel traction, the majority were steam operated to the bitter end. We are fortunate that they attracted the attention of many photographers, some anonymous some well known, and it is through their images that the life and times of the Irish narrow gauge can be relived. For me, the writing of these books and the collection of the pictures has been a voyage of discovery. I felt again and again that I was having the privilege of peeping back in time to an era long gone which I and my generation never had the chance of experiencing. If anything the fascination of these lines increases with the passing of the years, so perhaps this is the appropriate time to take this journey into the past – to the days when these wonderful railways were more than just a curiosity for tourists and played a vital role in the lives of the communities that they served.

The Cork, Blackrock & Passage line was unusual in that it operated a busy suburban service into Cork City. One of the railway's four 2-4-2Ts, No.7P, heads a train at the Cork terminus in Albert Street, not long before the line closed in 1932. Len's of Sutton.

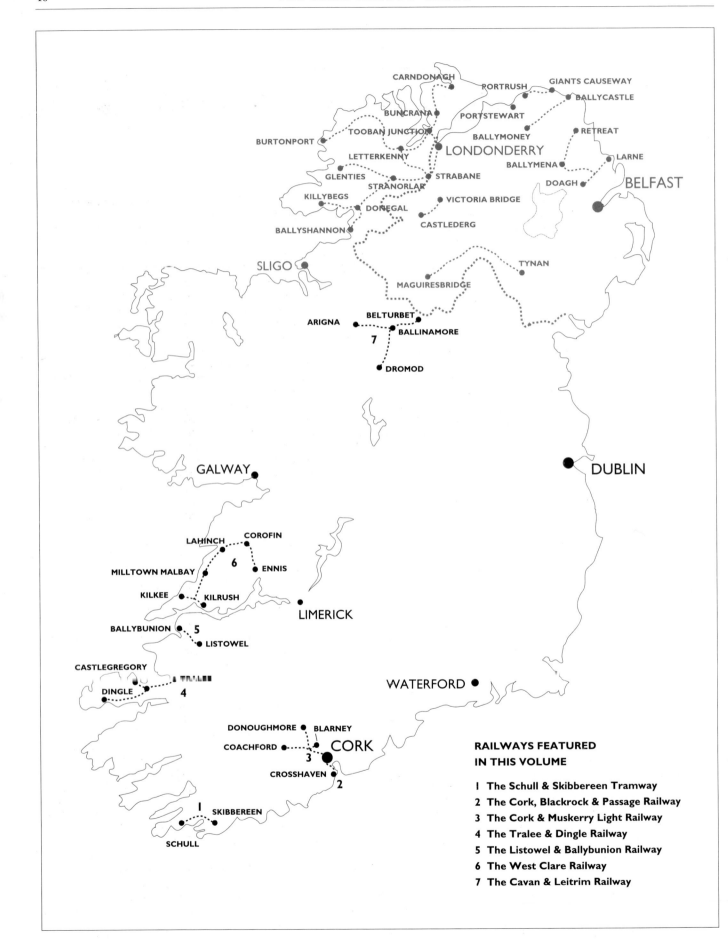

CARNDONAGH
RORTRUSH
GIANTS CAUSEWAY
BALLYCASTLE
BUNCRANA
PORTSTEWART
RETREAT
TOOBAN JUNCTION
BALLYMONEY
BURTONPORT
LARNE
LETTERKENNY
LONDONDERRY
BALLYMENA
GLENTIES
STRABANE
DOAGH
STRANORLAR
BELFAST
KILLYBEGS
VICTORIA BRIDGE
DONEGAL
BALLYSHANNON
CASTLEDERG
SLIGO
TYNAN
MAGUIRESBRIDGE
BELTURBET
ARIGNA
BALLINAMORE
7
DROMOD

GALWAY

DUBLIN

LAHINCH   COROFIN
MILLTOWN MALBAY   6   ENNIS
KILKEE   KILRUSH
LIMERICK
BALLYBUNION   5
LISTOWEL

CASTLEGREGORY
TRALEE
DINGLE   4
WATERFORD

DONOUGHMORE   BLARNEY
COACHFORD   CORK
3
CROSSHAVEN
2

1   SKIBBEREEN
SCHULL

RAILWAYS FEATURED
IN THIS VOLUME

1 The Schull & Skibbereen Tramway
2 The Cork, Blackrock & Passage Railway
3 The Cork & Muskerry Light Railway
4 The Tralee & Dingle Railway
5 The Listowel & Ballybunion Railway
6 The West Clare Railway
7 The Cavan & Leitrim Railway

Chapter One

THE SCHULL & SKIBBEREEN TRAMWAY

THE REMOTE Mizen Peninsula in the south west of Cork, Ireland's largest county, was the location of one of the first narrow gauge lines to be promoted under the provisions of the Tramways Act of 1883.

From the opening of the Cork & Bandon broad gauge line in 1851, the tracks of what was, through the amalgamation of a number of smaller companies, to become the Cork, Bandon & South Coast Railway, were gradually extended. The railway penetrated as far as Skibbereen in July 1877, stimulating interest in the promotion of railways to serve the remote districts to the east and west of that town. This was encouraged by the prospect of baronial guarantees as authorised by the Tramways Act.

A company called the West Carbery Tramways and Light Railways Ltd was set up in 1883 to build two lines from Skibbereen. One was to go east to Glandore with a possible future extension to Clonakilty. (The latter was in fact rail connected by a branch of the broad gauge from 1886 on). This eastern section was never built but the line to the west of Skibbereen, which became in time the Schull & Skibbereen Tramway, was originally planned to go to near the end of the Mizen Peninsula to terminate at Crookhaven.

The Cork County Grand Jury would only give a guarantee on the line to Schull when the scheme came before them in March 1884, though in hindsight to guarantee the interest on £57,000 of the company's proposed capital of £95,000 was very generous especially given the remote and depopulated areas which the planned line was to serve.

The relevant Order in Council authorising the line was issued in March 1885 and construction began shortly afterwards. The Schull line was in many ways the archetypal Irish roadside tramway. It followed the road for most of its route and this led to sharp curves and gradients as severe as 1 in 28 in places. The major engineering work on the line and one which can still be admired to this day, long after the passing of the railway, was the magnificent twelve arched masonry viaduct at Ballydehob, over the waters of an inlet of Roaringwater Bay. Ballydehob was the only village of any size

on the route of the line yet its station was some distance from the village it allegedly served.

Construction of the 15½ miles from Skibbereen to Schull took two years and later investigations revealed that the contractors had made a pretty poor job of it. Apart from the station at Ballydehob, which was also the only passing place on the line, halts were provided at Newcourt, Church Cross, Hollyhill, Kilcoe and Woodlands, though of these only Hollyhill had a building. The other stations offered short platforms without shelters. The completed line was inspected by Major General Hutchinson of the Board of Trade in August 1886. He was obviously unimpressed by what he saw as he refused to pass the line for public service. He made a second visit in September and allowed traffic to commence, though one senses with a certain reluctance, as he imposed a maximum speed limit of 15 mph. Things were clearly not as they should be for the service was suspended by the Company for ten days in October due to problems with the locomotives and the permanent way. The service, when it was running, consisted of two trains daily with an extra one on Thursday, which was market day in Skibbereen. The journey time for the 15½ miles was 1 hour and 20 minutes.

At first the Company had hoped that its line would be worked by the C&B but this was not to be so it ordered its own locomotives and rolling stock. Three 0-4-0T tramway locos were acquired from Dick Kerr & Company. These engines had their wheels and motion enclosed in the normal tramway fashion. They were troublesome and underpowered and rode badly on the poorly laid track.

Services were again suspended in April 1887. Some ratepayers in the county were even at this early stage in the tramway's history so exasperated at having to bail the Company out, that they made representations to the Lord Lieutenant which resulted in yet another visit from Major General Hutchinson. His report was pretty damning. It highlighted problems with the locomotives, turntables, the permanent way and the formation and made it clear that its author had little confidence in the

way the line was being maintained and operated.

To put matters to rights more money was borrowed and a new locomotive was bought. This was a 4-4-0T built by Nasmyth Wilson and supplied in 1888. Numbered 4 and named *Erin,* this engine was the first in Ireland to have the distinctive Belpaire firebox, named after the Belgian engineer who invented it and which was used on locomotives all over the world in the years following its introduction, in the 1860s, in its inventor's home country.

Losses on the Schull line continued up to 1892 when the Grand Jury appointed a Committee of Management. The West Carbery in effect lost control of its line to this committee which adopted the title for the concern by which it is most commonly known, the Schull & Skibbereen Tramway and Light Railway. October 1893 saw the opening of the only extension to the railway when a short branch to the pier at Schull was completed. All thoughts about the longer extension of the line to Crookhaven had been put aside by this stage.

Two unusual operating features of the line are worth noting. At Schull the engine shed was at right angles to the running lines and could only be reached by a turntable whilst at Skibbereen the narrow gauge station was on a cramped site adjacent to the broad gauge one. The line ended in a terminal bay platform and this meant that all departing trains had to reverse out of the station and into a head-shunt before heading off in the direction of Schull to the west.

The line acquired two further locomotives, one in 1906 and the other in 1914. Both were 4-4-0Ts supplied by Peckett. The last of the original 1886 tram engines survived until 1926. The 1906 Peckett was given the number 1 from the line's first engine which had by then been scrapped. The new No.1 was named *Gabriel.* The second Peckett became No.3 and was later given the name *Kent.* The final addition to the locomotive fleet arrived in 1938 when No.6K, a 0-4-4T from the recently closed Cork & Muskerry line was transferred to Skibbereen.

It was calculated that between 1886 and 1922 the S&S incurred losses of £152,755. This was made up of both operating losses and the payment of the baronial guarantees. In 1925 the line was taken over by the GSR under the reorganisation of the railways in the new Irish Free State and the rate payers of West Cork were at last relieved of their burden. The S&S section of the GSR carried on uneventfully until 1944. It avoided the fate of County Cork's two other narrow gauge lines in the 1930s but it became a minor casualty of the Second World War in April 1944, when the severe shortage of coal in Ireland caused the suspension of services. The line reopened in December 1945 but the shortage of coal continued and services were again suspended, this time for good, on 27th January 1947. By this time the line was in the control of CIE who substituted buses and lorries for the trains. The last act in the history of the Schull & Skibbereen came in September 1952 when the line was formally abandoned by CIE.

Left: **For the opening of the line three 0-4-0 tramway locomotives were ordered from Dick Kerr & Company. Numbered 1 to 3 they bore the names *Marion, Ida* and *Ilen*. As built they had cylinders of 9in by 16in, a wheelbase of 6ft and 2ft 6in diameter coupled wheels. Their well tanks held 350 gallons of water and they weighed 15 tons. They were equipped with condensers to deal with exhaust steam and in accordance with the stiff Board of Trade regulations of the period, their motion was covered with metal skirts, to within a few inches of the rails. Apparently rough riding and certainly prone to breakdowns, they were supposed to be capable of hauling 30 tons up a 1 in 30 gradient: this they were incapable of doing. No.1 was withdrawn in 1906, No.3 *Ilen*, seen here at Skibbereen in the early years of the century, lasted in its original condition, until 1914.**
Walter McGrath collection.

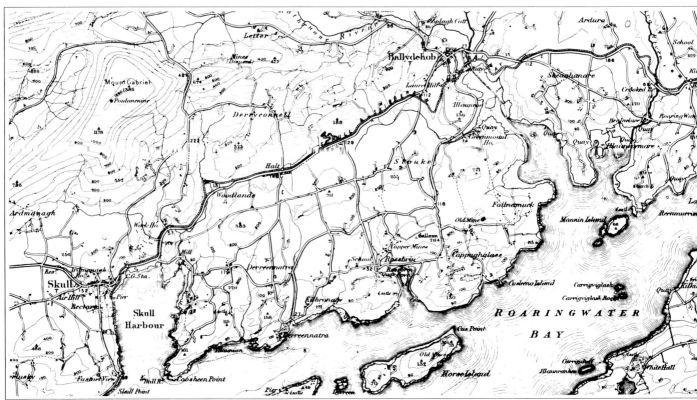

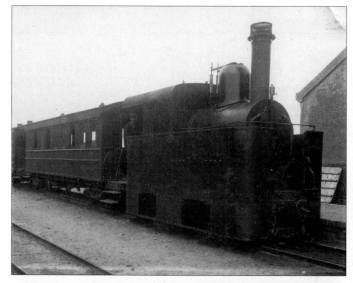

Above left: **No.2 *Ida* was extensively rebuilt in 1905. Its overall roof was cut back, a steam dome and Salter safety valves were fitted and in this condition it lasted until 1926.** Walter McGrath collection .

Above right: **By May 1924 No.2 had lost some more of its tramway skirts revealing its small wheels and part of its motion to the camera.** Ken Nunn collection.

Left: **The Dick Kerr locos gave endless bother. In 1888, to try and improve matters, a new and more powerful locomotive was purchased from Nasmyth Wilson. This was No.4, a 4-4-0T with coupled wheels of 3ft 4in diameter and a much greater tractive effort than the existing locos. As built it had cowcatchers at both ends and the motion was enclosed. No.4 was named *Erin* and had the distinctive feature of a very high dome. No.4 was at Skibbereen on 29th May 1924.** Ken Nunn collection.

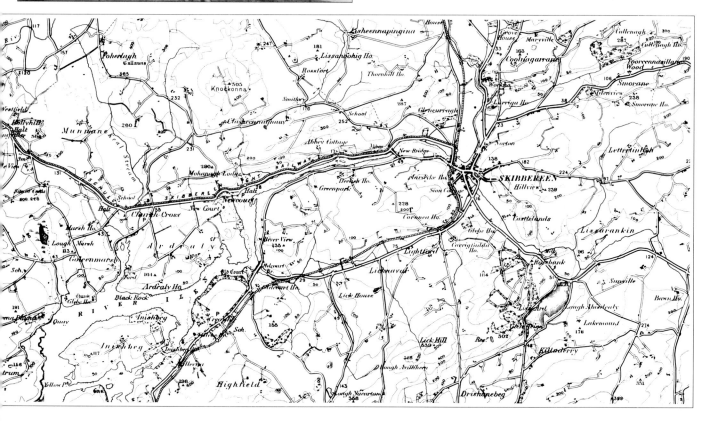

Top: **The S&S acquired two more locos in 1906 and 1914 respectively. Their arrival signalled the withdrawal of two of the Dick Kerr engines, one of which went in each of these years. Both new locos were Peckett 4-4-0Ts and took the numbers 1 and 3 of the tram engines they replaced. They were to be named *Gabriel* and *Kent*. The second No.1 *Gabriel* pauses for refreshment at the water tower outside Skibbereen shed on 16th September 1929.** H.C.Casserley.

Above left: On 16th September 1929 No.1 *Gabriel* shunts wagons towards the goods shed at Skibbereen. H.C.Casserley.

Above right: *Gabriel* was withdrawn in 1936 and from then until 1938 only two engines were available for service. To bring the establishment back up to three, in 1938 a 0-4-4T which had formerly run on the Cork & Muskerry line until its closure in 1934, was transferred to Skibbereen. This engine, built in 1893, had been dismantled and put

in store. It retained its old C&M number 6, to which was added the suffix S. No.6S was photographed by John Edgington outside the shed at Skibbereen on 7th July 1950, after services had been suspended for good.

Above: **The GSR quickly removed name and number plates from most of the narrow gauge locos which it took over in 1925. The S&S locos, with the exception of No.4, escaped this indignity. Because her name was painted on the side of her tanks and was not carried on a separate name plate, as was the case with the other engines, on her first visit to Inchicore, where heavy overhauls on S&S engines now took place, she acquired a standard GSR number plate and the name was obliterated. In this view, taken in the GSR era, No.4 is on the turntable at Skibbereen. The broad gauge wagons and the pile of boxes on the loading bank to the right of the engine, illustrates one of the drawbacks of having two gauges, the need to trans-ship goods and the heavy handling costs involved, not to mention the delays that this could cause.** Len's of Sutton.

Right: **No.3 *Kent,* named after an Irish patriot and not the English county, reposes outside Skibbereen shed on 1st July 1938. Strictly speaking the engine's number is now 3S. The GSR appended a letter after the numbers of their narrow gauge engines to indicate which section they hailed from. The 'S' was the letter applied to the Schull & Skibbereen section.** H.C Casserley.

Top: **The station layout at Skibbereen was most unusual. Trains to and from Schull could not run directly into the passenger platform but had to reverse in and out of a head-shunt. The train from Schull entering the station on the right will have to run up to the end of the head-shunt in the distance and set back to gain access to the passenger platform in the foreground.** H.C.Casserley.

Above: **In this general view of the station looking towards the head-shunt, the** platform and its bay are shown along with the ramshackle corrugated iron shed that provided some protection from the elements for prospective passengers. The building to the right is the carriage shed, at whose end, behind the camera, was located the engine shed. H.C.Casserley.

Left: **In this view of No.4 at the platform, the couture of the awaiting clients would seem to indicate the period as being the early 1930s.** Len's of Sutton.

Left: **These pictures of No.4 and her train at some of the various stopping places along the line were all taken by Henry Casserley on 1st July 1938. Where conditions permitted the tramway ran along the side of the public road. Typical of the roadside halts was Church Cross, 4 miles from Skibbereen. A platform was provided as was a shelter made of concrete with a corrugated iron roof. The train is the 12.00am mid day from Skibbereen.**

Below: **The next stop was Hollyhill, two miles beyond Church Cross. This had a station house, obscured by the train here, a siding and a loading bank.**

Bottom, far left: **A mile beyond Hollyhill was Kilcoe, where the return working, the 1.45pm from Schull pauses.**

Left: **Where the course of the road was too curved or hilly for the line to follow, it struck off on its own. Beyond Kilcoe, at a spot called Crooked Bridge, where there was once a halt, a water tower was located. With the water tank on its wooden plinth and the cow catcher on the engine, it is difficult to dispel thoughts of the 'Wild West' when looking at this picture.**

Left: **Ballydehob, some 10 miles from Skibbereen, was the only sizeable location along the course of the line. It was the only passing place, though this facility was rarely called upon, in GSR days at least, when the tramway was worked as a single section. The village was some distance from the station which possessed an island platform with a substantial station building and a large goods shed. Just beyond the station in the direction of Schull was the only major engineering feature on the line** and indeed one of the most impressive engineering works on the whole of the Irish narrow gauge. The massive twelve arched viaduct was built over an inlet of the splendidly named Roaringwater Bay and still stands today, well over forty years after the last train had run.
H.C. Casserley.

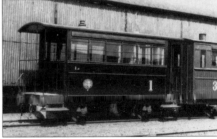

Above centre: **No.4 is on the 12.00am mid day from Skibbereen at Ballydehob on 1st July 1938. The goods shed is to the left of the train.** H.C.Casserley.

Left and above: **On the return working to Skibbereen from Schull later in the day, No.4 waits at the other end of the platform beside the goods shed. It will be noted from the coach behind the engine, seen in close up above, that even on a line as unassuming as this, class distinction was resolutely maintained. The 4-wheeled First Class coach with the end verandas dated from the opening of the line in 1886.**
Both H.C.Casserley.

Top: **At Schull the engine shed was at right angles to the running line and the only access to it was by means of a turntable. The line through the platform and the run round loop both converged on the turntable.** H.C.Casserley.

Above left: **The only extension of the line to be built was that to the pier at Schull. By the time it had been authorised by an Order in Council, granted in December 1892, the notion of extending the tramway further down the Mizen Peninsula to Crookhaven, had been dropped. A grant of £750 was obtained from the Treasury under the provisions of the Light Railways** (Ireland) Act of 1889, towards the cost of this short branch which appears to have been constructed by a separate entity called the Schull & Skibbereen Extension Tramway and Light Railway. The harbour line was ready by the Autumn of 1893. In this delightful picture, taken early in the twentieth century, of the pier at Schull, sailing vessels, horse drawn carts and narrow gauge wagons combine to make the most wonderful evocation of the methods of transportation available at the time. Walter McGrath collection.

Above right: **The line remained intact for a few years after the final suspension of services in January 1947. When it was eventually dismantled in the early 1950s, the remaining locos were loaded onto broad gauge wagons at Skibbereen and taken to Inchicore where they were broken up. The melancholy cortege is about to leave Skibbereen with No.6 on the leading wagon. No.4, minus chimney, but carrying her incongruously large dome to the very end, is on the one behind.** Walter McGrath collection.

Chapter Two

THE CORK, BLACKROCK & PASSAGE RAILWAY

THE CORK, Blackrock and Passage Railway shared an interesting distinction with two of Ireland's largest narrow gauge systems, the County Donegal and the Londonderry & Lough Swilly, in that the first part of its route was originally constructed to the 5ft 3in gauge and was later converted to the narrow gauge. It was, in its heyday, probably the busiest narrow gauge line in the British Isles and its first section out of Cork provided the only significant stretch of double track narrow gauge line in the country.

Cork City, situated at the mouth of the River Lee, is separated from the sea by a great natural harbour which takes its name from the city. Within Cork Harbour is the port of Cobh, from which in the days of the great Atlantic liners, tenders would set out to meet the ships in the open sea beyond. From the early nineteenth century a network of steamer services grew up serving various destinations within Cork Harbour, conveying goods and passengers and an increasing number of excursionists.

The port of Passage West (usually referred to as just Passage), was located a short distance across the water from Cobh.The route via Passage was the shortest way to Cobh and it is not surprising that the attention of railway promoters turned to a line from Cork to Passage. A line between these two places was authorised by Parliament as early as 1837 though it was not built at that time. This scheme was revived in 1840 and again sanctioned by the legislature. This time the line was built and two of the great figures of the early years of Irish railways were involved. Sir John Macneill was its engineer and William Dargan was engaged as the contractor for the last section into Passage. Public services began on 8th June 1850. Motive power for the whole of the line's broad gauge existence was provided by three 2-2-2 well tanks supplied by Sharp Brothers in 1850.

As well as running its railway, the CB&PR operated steamer services to a variety of destinations in Cork Harbour. The Railway's steamers were in fact run by its Directors in their private capacities as there was no provision in the Act authorising the line, for it to run steamer services. This anomaly was not put right until 1888 when

a new Act gave the Company the appropriate powers. The line prospered though it suffered severe competition for its Cobh traffic from 1862 onwards when a branch of the Cork to Youghal line was opened to Queenstown (as Cobh was formerly known). This forced the CB&PR to reduce its fares. A new city terminus was opened in 1873 at Albert Street near the Albert Quay station of the Cork & Bandon Railway.

Over the years the Directors of the CB&P reflected that their line was too short to be very remunerative, it being less than 7 miles from Cork to Passage. Thoughts began to turn to extensions of the route. The original plans had included an extension of about 1½ miles to Monkstown but this had never been built. Finally, nearly 50 years after the original line had opened, the Directors took the plunge and in 1896 the Cork, Blackrock and Passage Extension Act was passed which enabled the line to be extended a further 9½ miles to Crosshaven. At the same time the decision was taken to convert the whole line to the 3ft gauge. It was calculated that this would save £30,000 on the costs of the new line. The extension to Crosshaven was a difficult and expensive line to construct. It involved several major engineering works including a 500yd tunnel between Passage and the next station Glenbrook and a large four span lattice girder viaduct near Crosshaven.

Just at the time that the CB&PR was committing itself to the major expenditure of the Crosshaven extension, its lucrative commuter traffic into Cork from Blackrock was being threatened by an extension of the city's electric tramway system. The decision had been made to double the Cork to Blackrock section on conversion to the narrow gauge and this provided the only double track section of 3ft gauge line in Ireland. It was a reflection of how different the CB&PR was from the rest of the narrow gauge lines on the island. This was a busy suburban line serving a sizeable city not a rural tramway meandering through remote countryside.

The last broad gauge train ran in October 1900. To work the new gauge four 2-4-2T locomotives had been ordered from Neilson Reid in Glasgow. These were numbered 4 to 7 carrying on the numerical

sequence from the old 5ft 3in gauge engines which had been numbered 1, 2 and 3. The driving wheels of the 2-4-2Ts were 4ft 6ins in diameter, the largest found on any Irish narrow gauge engine. No further locomotives were bought up to the closure of the line. With their large driving wheels these were excellent and nippy engines, and speeds of up to 50mph were not unheard of. The narrow gauge coaching stock was supplied by the Birmingham firm of Brown Marshall.

The line to Crosshaven was soaking up a lot of capital. At first £80,000 in shares and £26,000 in loans had been raised but this had been used up by 1901 and a loan of £65,000 had to be negotiated from the Public Works Commissioners. It will be noted that at least the line to Crosshaven was funded on a commercial basis and was not dependent on the baronial guarantees upon which so many of the Irish narrow gauge lines constructed since the 1880s had had to call upon. In early 1902 the tunnel at Passage was at last completed and the first part of the new line, that from Passage to Monkstown was opened for traffic on 1st August of that year. Work continued on the section to Crosshaven which was finally opened on 1st June 1904 by the Lord Lieutenant. The final cost of the Crosshaven line was £200,093 – much more than had originally been anticipated.

The summer timetable of 1905 offered what was probably the most intensive service ever run on an Irish narrow gauge line. The regular service was hourly but on Sundays, between 9.30am and midday, a thirty minute frequency was provided to Crosshaven. This was to cater for the large number of day trippers who wished to visit the coast or take to the waters of Cork Harbour. This service required the use of all four engines and there was nothing in reserve in case of a failure. In 1906 up and down business trains were inaugurated with only one stop in each direction at Carrigaline. The up train left Crosshaven at 9am and took 36 minutes for the 16 mile journey to the city; the down service left Albert Street at 5.35pm. and took one minute less.

The CB&PR prospered in what seems in retrospect, to have been that Edwardian golden age enjoyed by the railways of the British Isles, for each summer the regular traffic was greatly supplemented by the excursionists' exodus to the coast. All this came to an end in August 1914 when war came. Cork Harbour was of significant strategic importance to Britain, which had a large naval base at Haulbowline and four military forts nearby. Shortly after war had been declared the military authorities closed Crosshaven station and the surrounding district to passengers and the Company's trains and steamers were pressed into service to deal with the heavy traffic generated by the increased naval activity at Haulbowline. The CB&PR's heavy excursion traffic was severely proscribed and the Company suffered considerable financial hardship as a consequence.

By 1916 interest payments on the Government loan of 1901 could not be met. The military restrictions and the higher costs for coal and wages contributed to this situation. Some respite came in 1917 when the Government took control of all Irish railways. An Executive Committee formed of railway managers was set up to control the network and negotiations began with the Government to obtain compensation for the various railway companies for the disruption caused by the war. 1918 was a year of record receipts for the CB&P of some £45,000 and ominously, record expenditure of £38,000. Much of the revenue resulted from the very heavy passenger traffic to and from Haulbowline and the other dockyards along the route. So great was this that the Railway Executive transferred five passenger coaches from other lines at this time and an old 1881-built

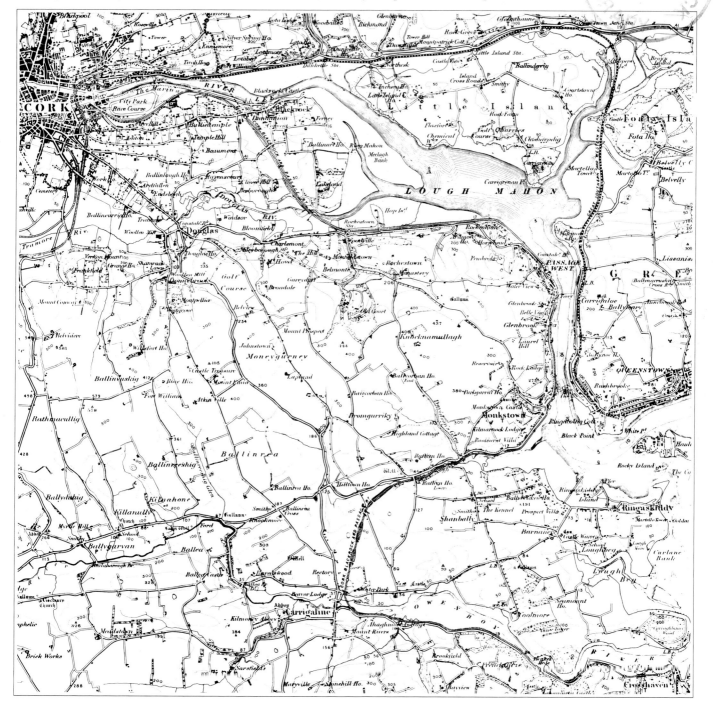

Sharp Stewart 2-4-0T which came from the County Donegal Railways.

The first summer of peace saw restrictions on coal supplies with priority being given to workers' trains. This greatly disrupted the summer services and much of this traditional revenue was lost. The distant horrors of the Great War and its more immediate economic ramifications were followed in the early 1920s by the disruption and destruction of the Irish Civil War.

Free State forces landed at Passage to take the city of Cork which was for a time held by republicans. The CB&PR had to endure a catalogue of destruction. The viaduct at Douglas was sabotaged, signal boxes were burnt out and the workshops at Passage were damaged. The result of the attack on the viaduct was that rail services were suspended for eight months. The Company's steamer services, which had finally been ended in 1921 were hastily reinstated as a stop gap measure. As peace returned to the country following the end of the Civil War, the railway was patched up and services were gradually restored to normal. But the CB&PR did not have much time left as an independent concern for the Free State's government had determined to unify the country's railways and on 1st January the Company became part of the GSR.

The CB&PR had made losses in 1923 and 1924 and this was a portent of what was to come. The GSR era was not a happy one for the line. Increasing bus and lorry competition caused a haemorrhage of traffic from the line. In 1927 the double track section from Cork to Blackrock was singled to save money. The all conquering motor bus led to the abandonment of Cork's electric tramways in September 1931. It is ironic that the trams which had filched so much of the railway's suburban traffic at the turn of the century were abandoned before the trains. But if this was a victory for the railway it was a pyrrhic one, for the GSR announced the closure of the line due to continuing losses, in 1932. The section from Monkstown to Crosshaven went first on 31st May, followed in September by the rest of the line: the last train leaving Albert Street on the 10th.

Thus after eighty two years and two gauges the CB&PR finally succumbed. Its character and traffic patterns had been very different from that which one normally associated with the Irish narrow gauge. It was suburban whereas all the rest were rural. It offered relatively frequent and, by narrow gauge standards, fast trains but its fate was sealed by road transport just as surely as was that of the other lines.

The line was outlived however, by its speedy and powerful 2-4-2Ts as we shall see when we meet them again on the Cavan & Leitrim line to which they were transferred by the GSR on the closure of the CB&PR.

Above: **The broad gauge makes one of its rare incursions into these pages in the form of these rare views of the CB&PR when it was a 5ft 3in gauge line. The CB&PR possessed three broad gauge locomotives which were in turn replaced by four narrow gauge engines. The engine illustrated here is one of the three 2-2-2Ts delivered by Sharp Stewart in 1850. They had 5ft driving wheels and the leading and trailing wheels were of 3ft 6in diameter. The polished brass domes incorporated the safety valves. As built they had no cabs which were later added by the CB&PR. One of the trio was at some stage in its career fitted with a saddle tank. The other two did not have this feature, which allows us to identify the engine on the passenger train near Cork as being No.2.**
Walter McGrath collection.

Above right: **This broadside view of No.2 shows her extremely antiquated appearance. She has brake blocks acting on either side of her driving wheels which is unusual and if you can imagine the cab and the saddle tank not being there, you could be looking at an engine from the dawn of the railway age.**
Walter McGrath collection.

Below: **On 15th September 1929, the other member of the quartet, No.4P, has been taking water at the end of the platform.**
H.C.Casserley.

Opposite page, top: **In the early years of the century a narrow gauge train has just left Passage station and is heading through the streets of the town towards the tunnel. This, the only one on the Irish narrow gauge, was 1,500 feet long and just beyond its southern portal was the next station, Glenbrook. During the course of its construction a spring was encountered which gave the contractor considerable difficulty and delayed the opening of the line to Crosshaven. A flagman is walking in front of the train to shepherd it through the streets until it regains its own right of way. Adjacent to Passage station was a pier at which CB&PR steamers called for many years. In the distance across the water is Great Island on which was located the important port of Cobh, or Queenstown as it was called at the time when this picture was taken. Among other claims to fame, this was the last port of call for the ill-fated Belfast built liner Titanic, on her maiden and only voyage, in 1912.**
Walter McGrath collection.

Opposite page, bottom: **Taken in GSR days at the line's Albert Street terminus in Cork. The GSR added the suffix P to their original numbers though they retained their cast number plates which were affixed to the tanks. Near the end of services in June 1932, reading from right to left, Nos 6, 5 and 7 pose for the camera of Henry Casserley.**

We will take a look in some detail at the four 2-4-2Ts which operated the fastest and most intensive service on the Irish narrow gauge. They were ordered from Neilson Reid of Glasgow in 1899 and delivered the next year. Weighing 39 tons, they had a tractive effort of 10,920 lbs and cylinders whose dimensions were 14½ by 22 inches. The CB&PR was primarily a passenger line and their 4ft 6in driving wheels enabled them to run at speeds, which for the narrow gauge, were high. On the closure of their own line they were sent to the Cavan & Leitrim section of the GSR. On the face of it this was about as different in character to their own line as any in Ireland could be. However they performed well in the north and we will meet them again in the C&L chapter of the book. Two of them lasted until that line's closure in 1959.

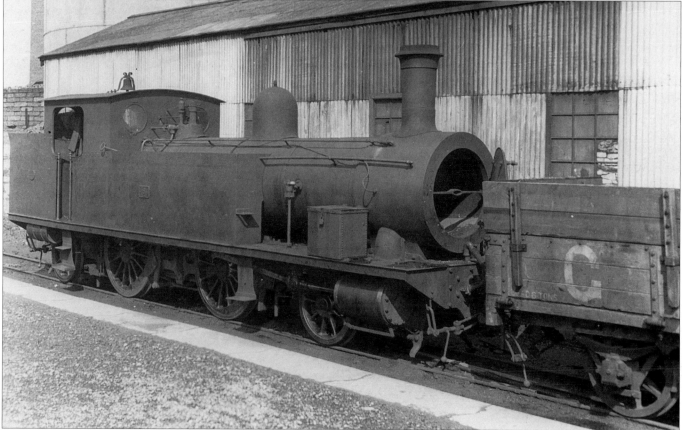

Opposite top: **No.4 was getting some attention from her fireman at Albert Street on 24th July 1914.** By this time events were well under way across Europe that led to the cataclysm of the First World War. Four days later Austria was to declare war on Serbia. The war accelerated the development of the internal combustion engine which was ultimately to have such a profoundly adverse effect on Ireland's narrow gauge lines. I wonder if events at the other end of Europe were discussed by the crew of No.4 on that sunny summer's day so long ago? Ken Nunn collection.

Opposite bottom: **On 25th July 1914 a gleaming No.5 heads the 3.30pm departure for Crosshaven.** CB&PR locos in the narrow gauge era were painted in a lined black livery which, when clean, as in this instance, can look superb on a steam locomotive.
Ken Nunn collection.

Top: **No.7 is pictured in this broadside view at Albert Street on 15th September 1929. Standards of cleanliness had obviously slipped since the previous picture was taken.** H.C.Casserley.

Above: **No.6 is in need of some attention in this 1920s view taken at Albert Street.** Len's of Sutton.

Left: **The only stretch of double track narrow gauge railway in Ireland is featured in two of these pictures. The decision to double the Cork to Blackrock section was taken when the extension to Crosshaven was being planned. This reflects more than anything else the unique nature of the CB&PR in terms of the Irish narrow gauge. It was urban rather than rural in character. Its revenues depended on the carriage of people rather than cattle as was the case with many of the others. Rex Murphy's famous picture, reproduced here by the courtesy of Walter McGrath, shows a mixed train slowing for a distant signal at a spot known as the Crinoline Bridge, between Albert Street and Blackrock. The double track was singled by the GSR in 1927, the year after this picture was taken, as an economy measure. This was an ominous reflection of the changing traffic patterns which brought about the demise of the railway in 1932.**

Left: **The other view of the double track section shows the 8.45am train from Cork to Monkstown on 23rd July 1914. The engine is No.6.** Ken Nunn collection.

Below: **In GSR days a train for Crosshaven leaves Carrigaline. This station had a signal box on its island platform and a subway to allow access to the platform. The chimney of the signal box can be seen behind the main station building. The steps and railings leading down to the subway are also visible. The engine is No.4P.**
Photo, the late Rex Murphy, courtesy Walter McGrath.

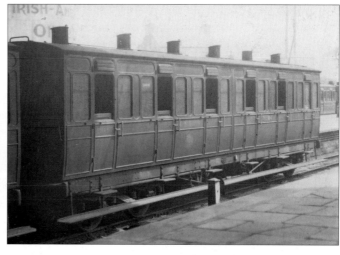

Top: The CB&PR suffered more than its fair share of damage in the troubles of the 1920s. In an attempt to impede the progress of Free State forces, who had landed at Passage to assert the authority of the new state in its second city, republicans blew up the Douglas viaduct near Rochestown station on 8th August 1922. Train services had to be suspended though the CB&PR substituted a steamer service in the interim. Buses are frequently used to replace trains when lines are under repair, but this is the only instance I can think of where this job was done by ships.

A temporary timber structure was fabricated by the Irish Army and the viaduct was fully restored to its previous condition by the end of 1923. This picture shows the first train over the temporary bridge supervised by some of the soldiers who had helped to construct it.
Walter McGrath collection.

Above left: 1922 was all in all a bad year for the line. In addition to the Douglas viaduct, two signal boxes were burnt down and a malicious fire seriously damaged the company's workshops at Passage,

destroying a number of coaches. On 28th May 1924, No.7 stands at Passage shed. This had been the site of the terminus of the original broad gauge line.
Ken Nunn Collection.

Above right: CB&PR coaching stock consisted of non-corridor bogie vehicles. No.24 seen here, was an all-Third. It was one of a number of carriages built by Brown Marshall for the rebirth of the railway as a narrow gauge line in 1900
H.C.Casserley.

Top: **We take our leave of this fine little railway with these contrasting images, taken within a few years of each other. No.7 prepares to leave Albert Street with a train for Crosshaven, a scene which had been repeated day after day for many years.** Len's of Sutton.

Above: **This delightful bogie First saloon was photographed at Albert Street early in the century, with two proud members of staff in attendance.** W.H.Butler collection.

Opposite page, top: **When Henry Casserley visited Albert Street on 10th June 1932, the first section of the line to go had already been closed ten days earlier. No trains ran on the Monkstown to Crosshaven stretch after the 31st of May so No.7 would be going no further than Monkstown.**

When Casserley returned to Albert Street two years later this was the sight that awaited him. The last service left on 10th September 1932. The once busy station is closed and in the process of being stripped of its railway artifacts. A ripped out water column lies beside a row of coach underframes, already stripped of their wheels and bodies. One of the all-conquering motor buses can be seen to the left of the train shed. These had accounted for Cork's electric trams even before the CB&PR closed. Railways take so long to build, but it seems it needs only the stroke of an accountant's pen to destroy them, as this picture so vividly illustrates.

Though abandoned railways became sadly commonplace to those of us growing up in the 1960s and '70s, there is still great poignancy in a scene like this. It must have been heart breaking for the railway workers who had kept the place in such good order, to see their efforts so quickly reduced to this.

Chapter Three

THE CORK & MUSKERRY LIGHT RAILWAY

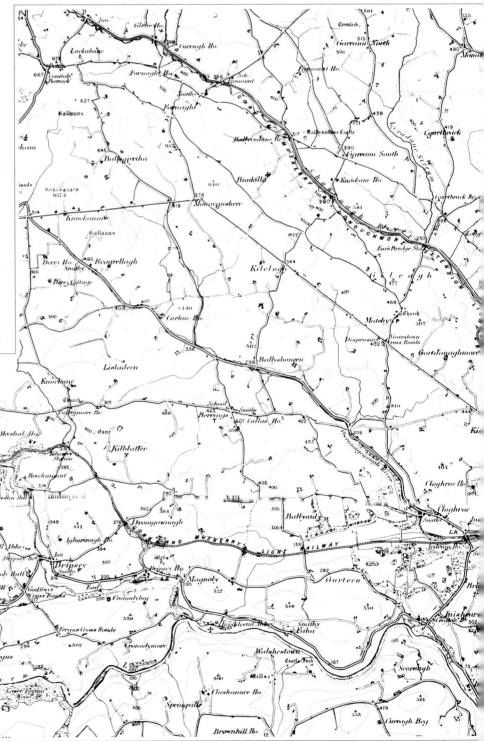

THE SECOND narrow gauge line which operated out of Cork City was rather different in character from the CB&PR, though it too had its separate terminus some distance from the heart of the city. For many years Cork had five railway stations, four of them termini, with no physical connection between any of them until the Cork City Railway provided a tenuous link between the Great Southern & Western Railway and the CB&SCR in 1912. The C&M was partly an urban line, partly a rural light railway but also a means of access to one of Ireland's leading tourist attractions.

The line was promoted in 1883 to open up the areas to the north west of the city including the barony of East Muskerry from which the line took its name. The promoters also had an eye for the potential tourist traffic to Blarney Castle where the kissing of the legendary Blarney stone was supposed to impart eloquence to those who risked breaking their necks by hanging upside down from the walls of the castle to do so. The line, which was to be 3ft gauge, was built under the aegis of the Tramways Act of 1883 under which baronial guarantees were sought. The scheme was approved by the Grand Jury in April 1884 and the procedures to obtain an Order in Council were commenced. The order had to be endorsed by an Act of Parliament and there were some difficulties with this; parliamentary approval was not given until June 1886.

A main line to Blarney was planned, with a branch to Coachford. The latter was about 15½ miles out of the city. The lines were to diverge at Coachford Junction. The junction was 6½ miles from the city and Blarney was another 2 miles on from the junction. Priority was given to the construction of the Blarney line which was built by the contractor Robert Worthington in a surprisingly short time. Work began in February 1887 and the line had been completed, inspected and approved by July of the same year. Public services began on 8th August with six trains daily. The city terminus was at Western Road and for the first 4 miles the railway followed the public highway. Work continued on the line to Coachford which was opened in March 1888.

The C&M system was completed by a branch off the Blarney line to Donoughmore. The Donoughmore Extension Light Railway was incorporated in 1889. The new line was to run for 8½ miles from St Annes, near Blarney, to the vicinity of the village in its title. It was nominally an independent concern but always worked by the C&M. Approved by the Privy Council in June 1891, this line opened for traffic in May 1893.

From its opening, up to the time of the Great War, the C&M prospered. It took tourists to Blarney, commuters in and out of the city and carried the produce and live stock of the districts it served. One interesting proposal from this period offered the prospect of through workings from the C&M to the CB&P over the tracks of the Cork city electric tramways. The gauge of the tramway was set at 2ft 11in. to allow railway vehicles to use it. Nothing came of this in the end but the prospect of narrow gauge steam trains progressing through Cork's streets would certainly have been a fascinating one for railway enthusiasts.

1913 was the C&M's most prosperous year with record receipts of over £11,000. In that year all the interest was paid from profits and no recourse was made to the baronial guarantees. The coming of war affected the C&M less dramatically than the CB&P. Indeed, when accounts came to be settled after the war and the Irish railways were being compensated for the effects of government control and the additional wear and tear which wartime demands on the railways had caused, the C&M did rather well. The Irish Railways Settlement of Claims Act of 1921 made up receipts of the railways to the level of 1913 and as this just happened to be the C&M's best year, they were not complaining.

Throughout its existence the C&M owned nine locomotives. For the opening of the line the Falcon Engine Works of Loughborough supplied three 2-4-0Ts, which logically carried the numbers 1, 2 and

3 and were named *City of Cork, Coachford* and *St Annes* respectively. The next engine was a solitary 0-4-2T from Kitsons. Smaller and lighter than the earlier trio, this engine, No.4 *Blarney,* was scrapped before the First World War. For the opening of the Donoughmore line two 0-4-4T locos were ordered from Thomas Green in Leeds. These were given the names and numbers, 5 *Donoughmore* and 6 *The Muskerry.* In 1898 the railway reverted to the 4-4-0T type for No.7 *Peake* built by the successors of the Falcon Engine Company, the Brush Electrical Engineering Company. The three original 2-4-0Ts had been rebuilt as 4-4-0Ts by this time. The penultimate C&M engine was another Brush built 4-4-0T No.8 *Dripsey,* similar to No.7 but less powerful than it. The last engine was ordered before the war but was only supplied in 1919. No.9 *Blarney* came from Hunslet but seems to have been rarely used and was scrapped as early as 1927.

The Civil War affected the C&M as it did the other narrow gauge lines in Cork. Over the years, extreme republicans seem to have taken particular pleasure in attacking railway lines and sadly this contribution to Ireland's progress continues to this day.

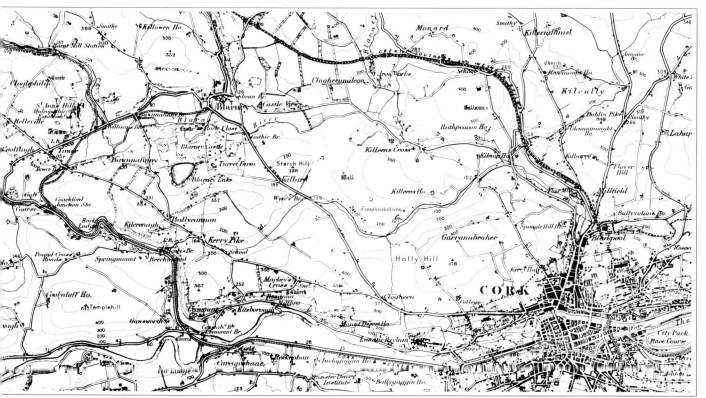

The destruction of a bridge over the River *Lee* at Leemount badly disrupted the C&M's services. When a railway is interfered with in this way its traffic has to find another way of getting through and once gone it tends never to come back. The same melancholy story we saw on the CB&P was being repeated here on the C&M. Civil unrest and the rise of the internal combustion engine reduced a once prosperous concern to a loss of £2,799 in its last year of independence. Taken over by the GSR in 1925, the line's new masters added the suffix K to the numbers of the lines engines to distinguish them.

Increasing road competition and contin-uing losses led to the almost inevitable announcement of closure and the last train ran on 29th December 1934. Of the remaining engines Nos 1,2,7 and 8 were scrapped. Nos 5 and 6 were dismantled and put into storage at Inchicore from where at least one re-emerged. No.5K was alleged to have been sent to the T&D where it was to become No.9T but I have yet to see any evidence that it ever went there. It may well have been scrapped at Inchicore instead. What is certain is that No.6 was sent to the S&S where it worked until the closure of that line.

The two narrow gauge lines out of Cork City were among the earliest casualties among the 3ft gauge lines of Ireland. Even though they served Ireland's third largest city, with, in theory, plenty of traffic on their doorsteps, I suppose in the case of the C&M it is hard to imagine steam trains processing down one of the main roads into the city for much longer than they did. Paradoxically it may have been their proximity of the city that was the cause of their downfall for the real killer of the Irish narrow gauge was road competition and there were plenty of buses and lorries around the city snapping at the railway's traffic. In the more remote parts of Ireland it took the motor vehicles longer to penetrate, thus giving the narrow gauge a longer innings.

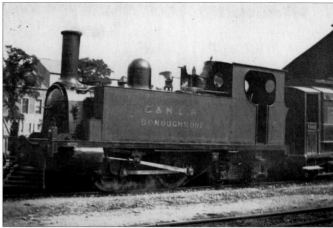

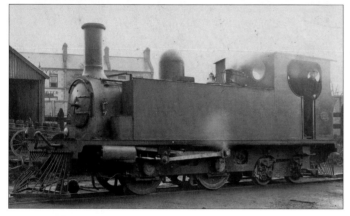

Of the nine locomotives owned by the C&M, we are able to present illustrations of all but one. The first three engines were delivered as 2-4-0Ts but, within a few years of the line's opening, they were rebuilt as 4-4-0Ts. All the locos were named after places served by the railway. The names were painted on the tanks and were dispensed with when the GSR took over in 1925. No pictures of the original trio of engines in the condition in which they were built seem to be extant, and one of these, No.3 *St Annes,* which was scrapped in 1923, even in its rebuilt condition seems to have been particularly camera shy.

Opposite page, top left: **No.1, originally named** *City of Cork* **and her two sisters were built by the Falcon Engine and Car Company of Loughborough in 1887. As delivered, these engines were 2-4-0Ts and had condensing gear and were fitted with skirts over their wheels and motion. Though these appendages were soon dispensed with, C&M locos carried bells and had cow catchers at the front until the line closed, because of the street and roadside running they had to do. The bell on No.1 can be spotted on top of the side tank. The loco was photographed during the GSR era, outside the main C&M engine shed, which was located at the Cork terminus in Western Road. Len's of Sutton.**

Opposite page, top right: **No.2** *Coachford* **is seen at Western Road on 4th September 1901. In C&M days the engines carried a light green livery. Nos 1 and 2 lasted until the line closed in 1934. Ken Nunn collection.**

Opposite page, bottom: **No.4** *Blarney* **was a strange looking 0-4-2 well tank supplied by Kitsons in 1888. This engine had been disposed of by 1911. It was less powerful than the other locos on the line and this may have been the reason for its early demise. A tall chimney mounted on a boiler set high to make space for the water tanks created the loco's singular appearance. Whether the**

picture of No.4 on the long train was posed or whether it could actually move a train of this size is open to debate. W.H.Butler collection.

Top left: **The first No.4, the Kitson 0-4-2T, had a short life by the standards of the Irish narrow gauge. Its replacement, which also was given the name** *Blarney* **had an equally undistinguished career, lasting a mere eight years. No.9 had been ordered from Hunslet before the war but was not delivered until 1919. What appears to be a second dome is in fact a sandbox. No.9 was scrapped in 1927, and in this rare picture, the engine is shunting at Western Road, on 28th May 1924. Ken Nunn collection.**

Top right: **To cope with the growing traffic on the existing lines to Coachford and Blarney and with the opening of the branch to Donoughmore imminent, two new locos were delivered in 1893. Nos 5 and 6 were built by Thomas Green and Sons of Leeds to the 0-4-4T wheel arrangement. They had outside cylinders and bearings and produced a useful tractive effort of some 11,100 lbs. On 26th July 1914, No.5** *Donoughmore* **is at the head of a train about to leave Western Road. Ken Nunn collection.**

Above left: **An 1890s picture of No.6** *The Muskerry.* **The definite article was later dropped from its name. W.H.Butler collection.**

Above right: **The success of the rebuilt 2-4-0Ts encouraged the C&M to go back to the Falcon Works at Loughborough, or as it had now become, the Brush Electrical Engineering Company, for their next two engines. No.7** *Peake* **was supplied in 1898 and No.8** *Dripsey* **arrived in 1905. This picture of No.7 in immaculate condition at Western Road must have been taken very soon after it was delivered. The loco displays one of the styles of lettering used by the company. Here it describes itself as the CMLR; in other instances it favoured the use of C&MLR. W.H.Butler collection.**

Photographs on the opposite page:

Top row, left: **No.8 *Dripsey* leaves with the 11.00am train to Blarney on 26th July 1914.** Ken Nunn Collection.

Top row, right: **Earlier that morning 0-4-4T No.5 was in charge of the 10.00am to Coachford. These two pictures will serve to remind us that three different destinations were served by C&M trains from this station.** Ken Nunn Collection.

Second row down: **In the GSR period No.5 enters Western Road with a short train. Just beyond this point the line took to the side of the road which it followed to the city boundary and on to Carrigrohane.** Len's of Sutton.

Third row down: **On Sunday 15th September 1929, No.5K leaves Western Road with the 10.30am departure for Blarney. The iron train shed was erected in 1898-99.** H.C.Casserley.

Bottom left: **In this 1920s view No.6 enters Western Road with another short train, evidence perhaps that the passengers were beginning to drift away.** Len's of Sutton.

Bottom right: **No.5 is turned on the turntable which was located at the city end of the Western Road site.** Len's of Sutton.

Above: **By way of contrast with the picture on the previous page, this is what No.7 looked like in GSR days. Weighing 28 tons, she was the biggest engine on the line and can be distinguished from No.8 because of the much larger dome she carried.** Len's of Sutton.

Below: **No.8, the former *Dripsey* at Western Road. Apart from her smaller dome both these engines were very similar in appearance.** Len's of Sutton.

Top and above left: **Shortly after leaving the confines of the station the trains began to run along Western Road itself. The road was shared between the C&M's steam trains, Cork City's electric trams and normal road traffic. In these two pictures of trains progressing along Western Road, the poles and supports for the tramways** overhead can clearly be seen, though by this time the city's trams had already been replaced by buses. The trams ran on the outside of the C&M tracks. H.C.Casserley.

Above: **On leaving the city boundary C&M tracks continued along the side of the public road. There was a long straight run of 2½ miles to Carrigrohane. The railway track was raised slightly above the level of the road. In this 1920s view, although the road is flooded, the train is able to get through.** Walter McGrath collection.

Above and left: **On this straight stretch of track, about halfway between Carrigrohane and Victoria Cross, occurred the legendary contretemps involving a Muskerry train and a steam roller. On 6th September 1927 the 7.45am mixed train from Donough-more was proceeding about its lawful business hauled by No.8, which had been named *Dripsey* by the C&M, when a steam roller engaged on repairs to the adjoining road, came into violent collision with it, derailing two bogie coaches. The impact broke away the front roller from the road vehicle and caused considerable damage to the train. These pictures bring to mind a fictitious encounter of a similar kind in the film, 'The Titfield Thunderbolt'. The derailed coach is No.7, a composite seating 40 passengers, supplied for the opening of the line in the 1880s. (Believed to be one of a batch built by Cravens of Sheffield.)**
Both Walter McGrath collection.

Top: **In this wonderful scene captured around 1909, an excursion from Coachford rounds the curve at Vagabond Rock between Coachford Junction and Healy's Bridge.**
Walter McGrath collection.

Above: **The modest station at Healy's Bridge between Leemount and Coachford Junction was typical of the intermediate halts on the C&M. The provision was probably more than adequate for the traffic on offer from such places.** Walter McGrath collection.

Above: **Coachford Junction was the point where the lines to Blarney and Donoughmore diverged from that to Coachford. This station had a signal box to control the junction and the corrugated iron structure seen in the picture to accommodate any passengers waiting for trains. The locomotive is either No.5 or 6 in original condition. The cow catchers at the rear of these locos were later removed.** Walter McGrath collection.

Above right: **Near the end of the railway's life, No.8K pauses at Coachford Junction on 9th July 1934 with the 12.05pm Cork to Blarney train.** H.C.Casserley.

Below: **St Anne's, where No.1 *City of Cork* was pictured, was the junction for the Donoughmore Extension Railway. Some trains ran through to Donoughmore direct from Cork. At other times the Donoughmore branch was served by trains to Blarney which, having gone there first, backtracked to St Anne's and then headed up the branch. Though theoretically an independent company, the DER was always worked as part of the C&M. At St Anne's there was a bay platform for Donoughmore trains and a turntable beside which No.1 poses in this picture, probably taken in the early years of the century.** W.H.Butler collection.

Above: **A rare view of the engine shed at Donoughmore believed to have been taken in the early 1930s. By this time the GSR had dispensed with the engines' names so the former *Peake* is now just plain No.7K.** Walter McGrath collection.

Top left: **We take our leave of the C&M with these views of Blarney station. The C&M station was much closer to the famous castle than that on the G&SWR main line to Dublin, some 1½ miles to the east. Constructed of the almost inevitable corrugated iron, the station building is still extant, as a public convenience, and the station yard is a car park for visitors to the castle.**

Top right: **On 9th July 1934 the 12.05pm from Western Road arrives at Blarney headed by No.8K, the former *Dripsey*.**

Above: **On 15th September 1929 No.5K is about to be turned at Blarney before its journey back to the city.** All H.C.Casserley.

Right: **For several months in 1932 Cork could boast a 15in gauge railway running only a few yards from the Muskerry track, but separated from it by a temporary wall at Carrigrohane Straight Road. The line, about half a mile in length, was one of the many attractions of the Cork International Industrial and Agricultural Fair, held from May to September 1932. Two German 4-6-2 miniature steam locomotives, named *Brangsch* and *Leipzig* and several open coaches were imported by sea to Cork for the exhibition, and were returned to Germany at its close. Thousands of people travelled over the line during their visits to the exhibition, using a temporary halt on the C&M section.** Walter McGrath collection.

Chapter Four

THE TRALEE & DINGLE RAILWAY

THE NARROW gauge railways of Ireland were a pretty mixed bag, ranging from short branch lines feeding into broad gauge routes, to complete and self contained systems like the CDR. If any one railway could be deemed to be typical of such a varied collection of lines, or if those interested in railways were asked to name the first Irish 3ft gauge line that came into their minds, I think the chances are that a lot of them would come up with the Tralee & Dingle.

The T&D represents the very best and the very worst aspects of the Irish narrow gauge. For the railway romantics it was situated in a wild, remote and beautiful part of Ireland and its trains had to cope with horrendous curves and gradients. The realists will note that it rarely earned enough to cover its working expenses, its operating practices were often slapdash and on occasions plain dangerous and that as early as the 1930s its services could probably have been dispensed with.

This was a line which would never have been built without the system of baronial guarantees set up by the Government. The T&D was originally sanctioned by the Privy Council in 1884 but the powers lapsed. They were renewed in 1888, in which year construction began. Of the £150,000 capital required to build the railway, £120,000 was guaranteed locally at 4%.

The T&D was promoted to open up the remote Dingle Peninsula to the west of Tralee, the county town of Kerry in the south west of Ireland. Tralee was already served by two broad gauge lines. The first of these, the Tralee & Killarney, opened in 1859 and provided a connection to the GS&WR's main Dublin to Cork line at Mallow. A branch of what later became the Waterford & Limerick Railway made an end-on connection with the GS&WR line at Tralee in 1880, having meandered through north Kerry from Limerick, over 70 miles from Tralee by rail.

Worthington, the contractor to the T&D, advocated that the 5ft 3 in gauge should be used. The use of the narrow gauge was not of necessity a condition of baronial support and in fact in the 1890s the GS&WR lines to Kenmare and Valentia Harbour, also in Kerry, were built to the broad gauge with the assistance of baronial guarantees. He was overruled on grounds of the extra costs involved. Work began in 1888 and it took three years to construct the 31¾ mile main line from Tralee to Dingle along with the 6 mile branch from Castlegregory Junction to Castlegregory, a small town on the shores of Tralee Bay.

The cost per mile was the astonishingly low one of £2,700. By way of comparison, when a few years later, the GS&WR line from Killorglin was extended to Valentia Harbour, where it vied with the rails on the pier at Dingle for the honour of being the most westerly railway in Europe, the cost per mile was over £8,600. The consequence of the T&D's low construction costs were to be found in gradients as steep as 1 in 29 and some very severe curves. The line was mostly unfenced and followed the road where it could and it crossed on the level over seventy roads or tracks. The original permanent way was very light at 45lbs per yard. It took several visits from Major General Hutchinson of the Board of Trade before he felt disposed to allow the line to be opened, which it eventually was, on 31st March 1891.

From the start of services, receipts failed to cover the working expenses and the unfortunate ratepayers had to subsidise the line. Ratepayers representatives demanded an enquiry from the Board of Trade and as early as March 1893 Hutchinson was back in Tralee presiding over this. The enquiry highlighted some malpractices and was shortly followed by an accident in May of that year at Curraduff where a train ran out of control on a steep downward gradient and was derailed with the loss of three lives. The accident was due in part to the negligence of the driver but was also put down to problems with the train's braking system. The accident seemed to confirm the worst fears of those protesting at the way the railway was being managed.

Under the terms of the baronial guarantee, if a railway failed to cover its operating costs for four years in succession, control of it passed to the Grand Jury. This fate befell the T&D in 1896. The Grand Jury set up a 'Committee of Management' to oversee the affairs of the railway but this made little or no change to the personnel who were running the railway or the methods that they were using. In the first year under the new regime ratepayers had to stump up £7,000 in subsidies for the line, a very substantial sum for the period.

One senses that the hostility to the T&D in its early years from the ratepayers may have been exacerbated by distaste for the landed gentry who had been instrumental in the promotion of the line. The railway's directors were drawn from this class and the Grand Jury, which dispensed the baronial guarantees, was the last official vestige of the power of the gentry. It must have seemed to the ratepayers that the folly of both building the railway and then mismanaging it was firmly at the door of the gentry whilst the price to be paid for their incompetence, fell to the ratepayers. The T&D was also a drain on government funds and following appeals from the Grand Jury for financial assistance in 1898 the Treasury made a one off payment to be rid of its responsibility for the line. This reduced the burden on the ratepayers though the subsidies that they had to shell out continued up to 1935. More public funding came in 1907 when a £23,000 grant from a government backed development fund allowed a deviation to the line to be made at the scene of the 1893 derailment at Curraduff and other improvements to be carried out.

The affairs of the T&D began to settle down in the first decade of the twentieth century though another bout of agitation by a Ratepayers Association in 1910 revealed serious deficiencies in the railway's accounts department. With the setting up of a system of democratically elected county councils in Ireland in 1898, much of the hostility previously directed at the Grand Jury and the directors of the railway, seems to have been defused.

The gradient profile of the T&D made it a very difficult line to work, though this in turn attracted great interest to the railway in its last years. Leaving Tralee, the first ten miles of track were reasonably level, in fact flooding caused by spring tides was an occasional nuisance on this stretch. The serious hill climbing began beyond Castlegregory Junction. In about four miles the line rose over 650ft on gradients of 1 in 29 and 1 in 31. Eastbound trains faced an extremely

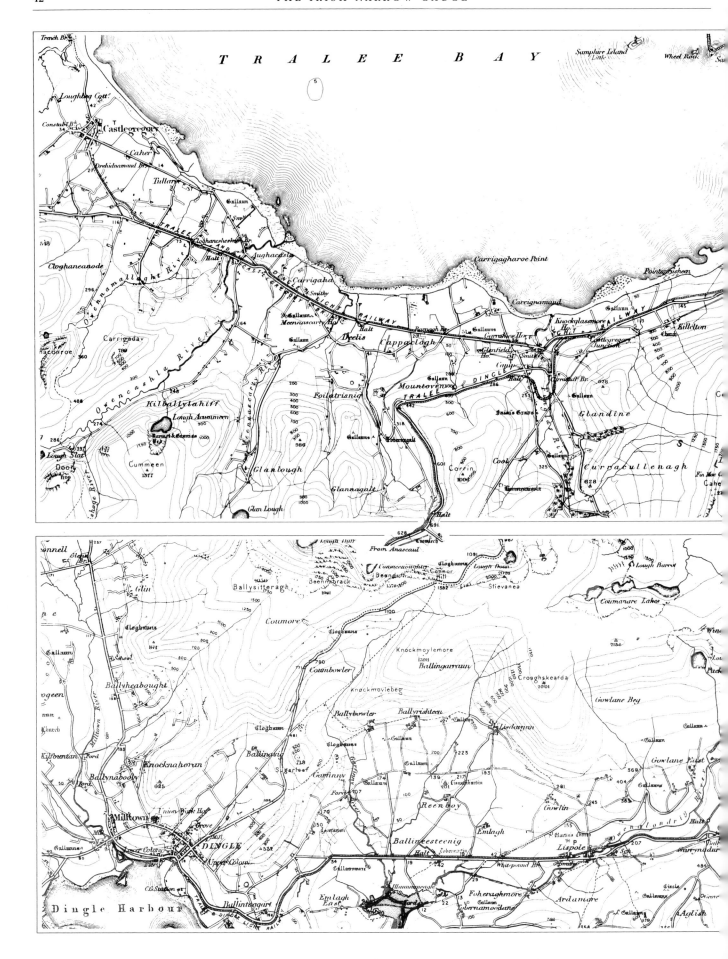

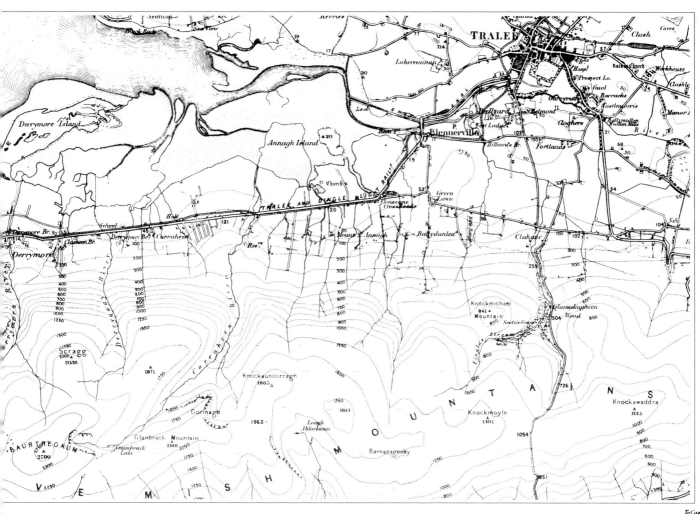

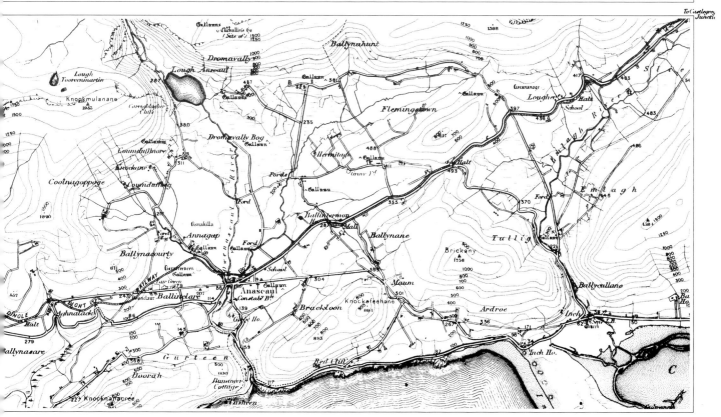

hazardous descent on this section in which occurred the Carraduff accident of 1893. The westbound climb to a summit at Glenagalt was followed by sharp westbound decent and then a climb to a second summit at Garrynadur. The drop from this summit ended on the middle of the famous Lispole Viaduct and also offered grades of 1 in 29 and severe curves. The last stretch into Dingle followed the road and was fairly level. Beyond Dingle station there was a short and steeply graded branch, down to the pier. This fell into disuse from the 1930s onwards. By contrast to the main line the Castlegregory branch was a very tame affair. It was the switchback nature of the middle section of the T&D which made the line famous.

To work this difficult road the T&D acquired, between 1889 and 1910, a total of nine locomotives. Seven of these were supplied by Hunslet, the other two were built by Kerr Stuart. One of the locos was a 0-4-2T, another was a 2-6-2T and all the rest were 2-6-0Ts. Three Hunslet 2-6-0Ts were delivered for the opening. Nos 1 and 2 lasted until the railway finally closed in 1953 whilst the third was transferred to the C&L in 1941 where it survived until that line was closed in 1959. In 1890 a small 0-4-2T was ordered from Hunslet for use on the Castlegregory branch. This engine, No. 4, had by the standards of the Irish narrow gauge, a very short life, being scrapped by 1908. The next engine was the unique Hunslet 2-6-2T supplied in 1892. No.5 had an adventurous career, being exiled to the C&L in 1950 and on the closure of that line it was saved for preservation in the United States. Some thirty years later it has been repatriated and overhauled for use on a stretch of its old line which has been rebuilt near Tralee.

The T&D reverted to the Hunslet 2-6-0T design for locomotive No.6 delivered in 1898. This engine escaped to the West Clare in 1953 and was sent north to the C&L in 1957 where it was scrapped when that line closed in 1959. The last three locos were all 2-6-0Ts. The first two of these were built by Kerr Stuart in 1902 and 1903 respectively. They were numbered 7 and 8 but when the Hunslet 0-4-2T No.4 was scrapped in 1908, its number was transferred to No.8. The final engine, which came from Hunslet in 1910, became the new No.8. For this reason, even though the T&D had a total of nine engines throughout its existence, the number sequence never went higher than No.8.

The relative stability which descended upon the T&D in the years before the First World War did not last long. The troubles which beset Ireland after the war were particularly felt in Kerry where the republican sympathies of many of the people were guaranteed to cause friction, with first the British authorities and later the new government in Dublin. The railway did not escape the disruption of the period. The British military closed the line in 1921 and services were again suspended for periods in 1922 and 1923. The Committee of Management which was still running the line, struggled manfully on but it must have been a relief for them to have had the line absorbed into the GSR in 1925. The new regime did not begin auspiciously, for on the day the GSR took over, 1st January 1925, a train demolished a Model T Ford at one of the many road crossings on the line.

The usual economies were put into effect with the workshop at Tralee being run down and locos sent to either Inchicore or Limerick for overhauls. The state of the roads in Kerry kept the T&D in business but little was done to renew the track which had had precious little attention since the line was opened. The crunch came in the late 1930s when the road to Dingle was resurfaced giving road transport an added impetus. In 1939 the bus to Dingle took 105 minutes, whereas the train running on life expired track with stops for shunting en route, took 155 minutes! On 17th April 1939 the GSR closed the Castlegregory branch completely and withdrew passenger services on the main line. Buses replaced the passenger trains and the railway was reduced to offering one goods train per day. The goods service continued throughout the war but was finally curtailed by the coal shortages in 1947. A rail service was eventually restored in the form of a monthly cattle train, run to coincide with the fair at Dingle. The fame of this remaining train began to spread and attract the attention of railway enthusiasts throughout Britain and Ireland. Some visitors came from Europe and the USA to see and travel on it. The cattle trains brought to the T&D, in its twilight years, fame and photographic coverage that it had never had in its heyday. These trains finally ended in June 1953 and brought the saga of the narrow gauge in County Kerry to a close, or so it seemed. Forty years later part of the T&D near Tralee has been relaid for the benefit of tourists to the area and locomotive No.5, the only 2-6-2T in the old T&D fleet, has been restored to working order to haul trains from Tralee to Blennerville. Whilst this may not offer the excitement of careering down from Glenagalt or storming across Lispole Viaduct to get a run at the bank beyond, at least it is pleasing to report that the 3ft gauge has once again got a foothold in the Kingdom of Kerry.

Maps on pages 42 and 43:

Opposite page, top: **The Tralee & Dingle acquired a fleet of nine locomotives at various times between 1889 and 1910. One of these was a short lived 0-4-2T, another was a 2-6-2T which is still going strong and the rest were 2-6-0Ts. The latter is an unusual wheel arrangement for tank locomotives, but it seems to have served the T&D well. Five of the seven 2-6-0Ts were Hunslet products. The first three of these (Works numbers 477-479) were supplied in 1889. No.1 is seen here at Tralee in GSR days.** Len's of Sutton.

Opposite page, centre left: **The second 2-6-0T is outside the original engine shed at Tralee on 24th July 1914. These engines weighed 38½ tons, had cylinders of 13 x 18ins and driving wheels of 3ft diameter. Some details common to many Irish narrow gauge engines may be observed on No.2. The engine has a single buffer/coupler with side chains for additional security, at the front. The cow catcher was an essential on a line like this which afforded livestock so many opportunities for trespass. A bell is fitted behind the dome though surely the noise made by the engine and its train would have drowned out its tocsin.**
Ken Nunn collection.

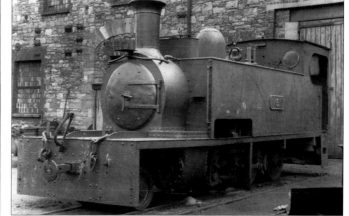

Centre right: No.3 was sent to the Cavan & Leitrim line in 1941 where it was a regular performer until the closure of that railway in 1959. Before this happened the engine was photographed on the mixed gauge track at Inchicore, probably in the early 1930s, painted in the GSR's dowdy grey livery. Len's of Sutton.

Right: The other 1889 Hunslet, No.3, lies out of use awaiting repairs at Tralee in 1914. Beside it is the hulk of No.1. This was the locomotive that was involved in the accident at Curraduff in 1893 when it became derailed on a viaduct and finished up, with much of its train, in the stream below. No.1 was later rebuilt and lasted until the end of services in 1953. Ken Nunn collection.

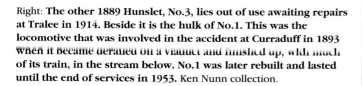

buffer beam is the GSR 'T' suffix for the line but it retains its original T&D number plate. No.4 went north to the C&L in 1941 and lasted until 1959. Len's of Sutton.

Centre left: A very rare early view of the unique Hunslet 2-6-2T No.5, which was built in 1892. This picture was probably taken in the 1890s. Compare this with the similar broadside view taken about sixty years later on page 86. The very large headlamp used in the early years of the line is notable as is the T&D number plate on the side of the tank. W.H.Butler collection.

Bottom: For its next engine the T&D reverted to the 1892 Hunslet 2-6-0T design. No.6, built in 1898, is seen in original condition outside the old T&D wooden shed at Tralee in 1914. Ken Nunn collection.

Below: This later picture of No.6 was taken in GSR days, outside the new shed, built in 1918 at Tralee. Len's of Sutton.

Above: The first No.4 was a light Hunslet 0-4-2T which was used mainly on the Castlegregory branch until it was scrapped in 1908. That engine's number was taken in 1908 by this Kerr Stuart built 2-6-0T, which from its arrival in 1903 until then, had been numbered 8. It is seen inside the shed at Tralee stopped for repairs. On its

Above: **No.7 was built by Kerr Stuart (Works No.800), in 1902. It was scrapped as early as 1928. Compare this with the Hunslet built 2-6-0T (right).** Ken Nunn collection.

Above: **The second No.8, which took the number of the other Kerr Stuart 2-6-0T that in turn became No.4 in 1908, was the last new engine ordered for the T&D. This Hunslet built loco lasted until the line closed when it was sent to the West Clare. It was rendered redundant and scrapped following the complete dieselisation of that line in the mid 1950s.** Len's of Sutton.

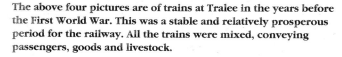

The above four pictures are of trains at Tralee in the years before the First World War. This was a stable and relatively prosperous period for the railway. All the trains were mixed, conveying passengers, goods and livestock.

Centre left: **The earliest view is that of No.2 waiting for the off on 3rd September 1901.** Ken Nunn collection.

Centre right: **On 24th July 1914 No.6 is on a train for Dingle. The first vehicle is an open topped cattle wagon. This is followed by** three goods vans and two of the line's twenty one bogie passenger coaches, probably an all-Third and a brake composite. Ken Nunn collection.

Bottom left: **On the same day, 24th July 1914, No.8 arrives with a train from Dingle.** Ken Nunn collection.

Bottom right: **That morning, No.6 leaves Tralee with the 8.30am to Dingle.** Ken Nunn collection.

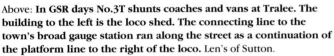

Above: **In GSR days No.3T shunts coaches and vans at Tralee. The building to the left is the loco shed. The connecting line to the town's broad gauge station ran along the street as a continuation of the platform line to the right of the loco.** Len's of Sutton.

Above: **On 6th July 1950, Nos.6T and 1T peep tentatively out of the engine shed at Tralee. By this time the monthly cattle special run in conjunction with the fair at Dingle, and its associated empty stock movements were their only employment.** John Edgington.

These scenes were recorded at Castlegregory Junction on 14th July 1934.

Left: **The 10.50am from Tralee to Dingle pauses at the Junction headed by No.5T, the Hunslet built 2-6-2T. The junction was fully signalled with the lower quadrant semaphores which found almost universal favour in Ireland.** Both H.C.Casserley.

Below left: **The connecting train to Castlegregory was headed by No.8T. Both passenger and freight services on this 6 mile branch were to survive only another five years. It was closed completely on 17th April 1939.** H.C.Casserley.

Below: **In the late 1930s, what is believed to be a sugar beet special, crosses the bridge over the Bunowa River on the Castlegregory branch, heading east towards the junction.**
Walter McGrath collection.

These pictures of what was almost certainly the last passenger train into Dingle, and one of the last trains of any kind on the line, in its last month of operation, June 1953, are included to give a flavour of the landscape of the Dingle Peninsula which the railway served. The photographs were taken by J.H.Price, who was the organiser, on behalf of the Light Railway Transport League and the Irish Railway Record Society, of an extensive tour of the remaining Irish narrow gauge lines. The locomotive on this occasion was No.8. See also page 112.

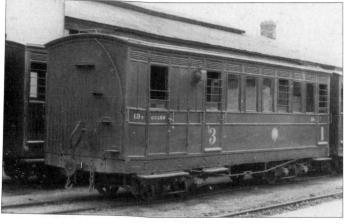

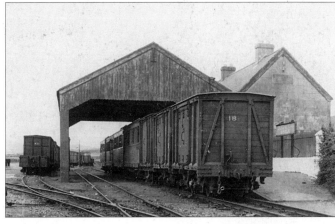

Opposite page, top: **One of the 2-6-0Ts makes up a train at Dingle in 1907. This is an interesting picture in that it shows the original station and engine shed. A wooden engine shed, not unlike that at Tralee which lasted until 1918, was replaced by one of stone construction in 1914. The old shed can be seen through the train shed at the end of the platform. The station building itself and the train shed were severely damaged by fire in the troubles in the 1920s. Our other pictures of Dingle show the station in its rebuilt condition.** Walter McGrath collection.

Opposite page, bottom: **No.5 is serviced outside the 1914 stone built engine shed.** H.C.Casserley.

Opposite page, centre left: **When Ken Nunn visited Dingle in 1924, the last year of the T&D's independent existence, the new train shed had just been completed. No.5 was the engine on duty for the 2.30pm to Tralee on May 30th.**

Opposite page, centre right: **On Henry Casserley's visit to Dingle, just over ten years later, on 14th July 1934, No.5 was again on duty. A GSR number plate has replaced the T&D one seen in the earlier picture. She is a tight fit for Dingle's turntable. The line to the left of the engine continued for about ⅓ of a mile down to the pier though by this time it had already fallen into disuse.**

Top and above left: **Most of the T&D's carriages were built by the Bristol Carriage and Wagon Company. One of the drawbacks for passengers on the line, apart from the amount of time spent shunting at stations, was the fact that in winter the carriages were unheated. In GSR days the suffix T was applied to coaches and wagons as well as to the locos. No.14T was a brake Third and No.13T was a brake composite with accommodation for both First and Third-class passengers.** Both H.C.Casserley.

Above right: **To cope with the severe gradients on the line, T&D goods vehicles were equipped with vacuum brakes. This enabled them to be mixed at random along with passenger carriages in the formation of trains.** H.C.Casserley.

The Tralee & Dingle became the responsibility of CIE in 1945. From 1947 until the line finally closed in 1953, the monthly cattle specials were the only traffic on the line. The fame of these trains spread and many railway enthusiasts came to ride on and photograph them. Our final pictures of the T&D fittingly feature these trains.

In the upper picture Nos 1T and 2T are approaching Castlegregory Junction from the rugged heights of Glenagalt with a loaded train from Dingle Cattle Fair. Walter McGrath collection.

The lower photograph, by the Dublin photographer Sean Kennedy, also taken in the final years, shows one of the cattle specials gingerly crossing Lispole Viaduct.

Double heading across the fragile viaduct was supposed to be banned, but by this stage in the game, nobody really minded.

Chapter Five

THE LISTOWEL & BALLYBUNION RAILWAY

No MORE singular line of railway was ever built in the British Isles, than that which ran from 1888 to 1924, linking the towns of Listowel and Ballybunion in County Kerry.

Ballybunion is a pleasant little seaside town in north Kerry, which in the 1880s was situated 9 miles from the nearest railway at Listowel on the line from Tralee to Limerick. All over the British Isles, small communities like this were anxious to be connected to the railway system, which was perceived in the nineteenth century, as the artery along which flowed prosperity. The town's first attempts to get a line built were conventional enough. In 1883 a 3ft gauge line was promoted by the Munster Steam Tramways Company. This was opposed by a rival scheme offered by the Limerick and Kerry Light Railways Company for a 5ft 3in gauge branch between the two towns. Both concerns sought baronial guarantees and this was enough to alarm groups of ratepayers in the area who realised that they would be left carrying the financial can, should the proposed lines fail to prosper. The Munster Tramways plan was rejected by the Privy Council in 1884, that of the L&KLR got as far as a committee of the House of Commons before it met the same fate in 1885.

From the railway politics of north Kerry our scene now shifts to the deserts of French North Africa where we first encounter Charles François Marie-Therese Lartigue, a French engineer working in his country's north African colonies. He was supposedly inspired to think about monorails by watching camels transporting goods carried on pallets or litters hanging on either side of their humps. He wanted to devise a system of railway construction that was light, flexible and cheap to build. It is worth taking a moment to describe his invention before taking our story any further.

Lartigue's monorail track consisted of a running rail supported on 'A'-shaped metal trestles. These trestles were anchored at the bottom onto iron or wooden sleepers. A metal brace, to give the system some rigidity, formed the cross bar of the 'A' and lighter rails ran along the outside of the trestles at the height of the cross bar, to stabilise the rolling stock. The trains ran on vertical double flanged wheels which bore all the weight, though horizontal double flanged wheels were fitted on either side of the vehicles to run on the lower rails. The horizontal wheels were there to control lateral movement. The triangular shaped track dictated triangular shaped trains as, by the very nature of the design, the track imposed itself into the middle of the vehicles, which were suspended from the top running rail, just like the pallets from the camel's hump.

The Lartigue system was first tried out in North Africa where it was employed in the collection of esparto grass, used in the manufacture of paper. This was transported across the desert in monorail wagons hauled by mules. The advantages claimed of it were that the track could be easily lifted and relaid, that it was quick to construct and that it was easy to operate. The system was next applied to an iron ore mine in south west France and it was exhibited at trade fairs in Paris, Rouen and Antwerp. A company was formed to exploit Lartigue's invention and, with an eye to it being used in parts of the British Empire, a remarkable demonstration was staged in London.

It is hard to believe today, but in the 1880s there was an area of waste ground in Westminster between Victoria Street and Birdcage Walk called Tothill Fields and it was here that the Lartigue monorail was demonstrated in 1886. Two lines were displayed, a light portable version and one of sturdier construction designed for permanent applications. The lines demonstrated all the features and potential advantages claimed for the system. They had grades of up to 1 in 10, sharp curves, trestles of varying heights to reduce the construction costs of the formation, turntables to switch trains from track to track and even a rack section.

The Lartigue Company wanted to establish a permanent line to display their system to its best advantage. You will remember that the railway promoters of north Kerry had seen their schemes failing to get parliamentary approval in 1885. Somehow or other, I cannot say precisely how or when, these two aspirations came together and a bill was promoted and a Company formed in 1886 to build a railway, from Ballybunion to Listowel, using the Lartigue monorail system. The line was to be constructed by the Lartigue Company at a cost of £33,000; significantly no baronial guarantees were sought. Work began in the autumn of 1887 and the line was opened in March 1888. It had been built very quickly and to budget which facts distinguish it from many other Irish minor lines of this period. Three 0-3-0 tender engines were supplied by the Hunslet Engine Company of Leeds, the only railway engines I have ever heard of which included an odd number in their wheel notation!

The usual service consisted of three trains daily with extras run in summer. The top speed was 20mph, the average was 15mph. Reports from those who travelled on the line remarked on the high noise levels inside the carriages. This is not surprising given the fact that passengers sat with their backs to the running rail, their ears a few inches from the wheels. One of the practical drawbacks of the system was the need to equalise the loadings on both sides of the vehicles. A cow carried on one side of a wagon would have to be balanced by a few sheep or pigs on the other.

The line did not prosper. Receipts in winter did not cover expenses and in 1897 it went into Chancery with its General Manager being appointed as Receiver. Almost inevitably the Lartigue system did not win any widespread support and in 1890 the Lartigue Company was wound up. The railway made small surpluses or losses between 1900 and 1913 in which year its profits peaked at a total of £875, though this was still not enough to pay interest on debentures. The line suffered some malicious damage in the Civil War and the financial position continued to deteriorate.

The end came in 1924. The L&B was not thrown the lifeline of amalgamation into the GSR. It is not unreasonable to assume that the latter, faced with the need to repair or replace such unusual locos and rolling stock, decided on that basis not to touch it. By October 1924 losses were running at £30 per week and a successful application was made to the High Court to close the line.

The last train ran on 10th October 1924, the track was quickly dismantled and sold for scrap. Thus ended one of the strangest railways ever devised. What is fascinating about the L&B is not just the Lartigue system itself but the fact that such an unconventional railway should have been built in the first place and operated for nearly 40 years in such a delightful but remote part of Ireland as north Kerry. It is hard to come to terms with the naivety or the blind enthusiasm of the promoters of the Lartigue Company who must have seriously expected potential customers from

around the world to make their way to Listowel to see the system in action. The fact that no one came and that the Lartigue system did not find customers elsewhere surely sealed the fate of the L&B to that of being a bizarre curiosity rather than the progenitor of a new direction in light railway technology.

Copyright reserved, Ordnance Survey, Dublin. Reproduced from 1 inch series, sheet 151; revised 1911; published 1913. Scale 1 inch to 1 mile.

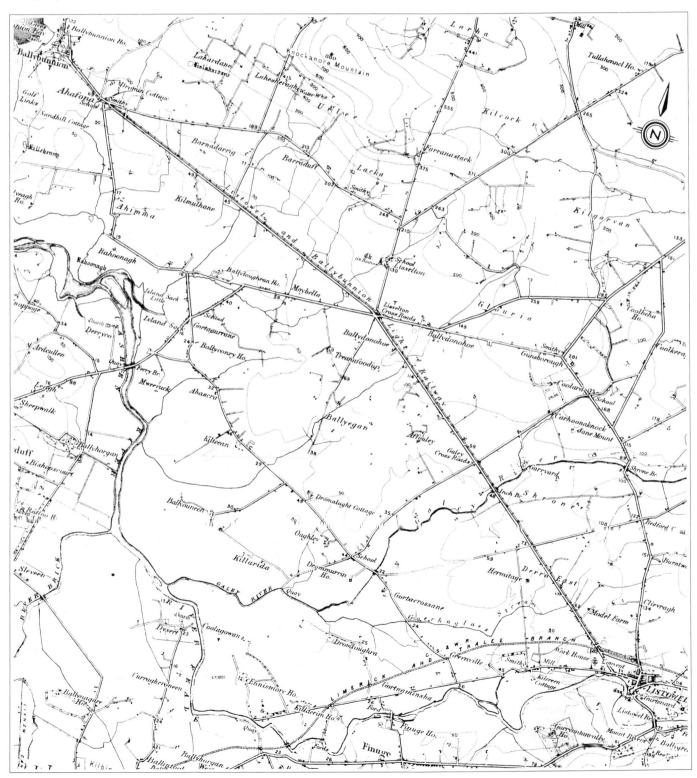

Top: **Framed in the foreground by a close up of the monorail track, 0-3-0 No.2 waits its next call of duty at Ballybunion.** W.H.Butler collection.

Above: **Locomotive No.3 has just arrived at Ballybunion from Listowel. The first vehicle with the built on cross rail steps, is what could loosely be described as a brake third, with accommodation** for the guard and some passengers. **The third vehicle is a set of wheeled cross rail steps which were to be found in the consist of most passenger trains. If there was no room on one side of the train, potential passengers could climb over the steps and try their luck on the other side of the tracks.** W.H.Butler collection.

Top left: **On 23rd July 1914 the 3.00pm departure from Ballybunion nears Listowel. Loco No.1 heads a train, consisting of two carriages, three wagons and one set of steps. I have always been very struck by the appearance of the carriages. On the outside they looked very similar to the conventional railway carriages built at the same time.** Ken Nunn collection.

Top right: **This is how the Lartigue system coped with the need to cross roads on the level. The line is protected by gates in the conventional way but the track itself rotates on a turntable to allow road traffic to pass through.** Kenn Nunn collection.

Above centre: **An unconventional line like this called for unusual solutions to some of the normal operational requirements which any railway has to meet. In this view of Ballybunion station one of the turntables which acted as points on the Lartigue system, is well illustrated.** Ken Nunn Collection.

Left: **Seventeen of these drawbridges or 'Flying Gates' as they were described, were erected along the course of the line to allow local traffic to pass over it. In this picture the man is manipulating the chains that will lower the bridge, whilst the donkey's gaze is fixed resolutely on the other side.** Courtesy *The Railway Magazine.*

Right: **No.1 takes water at Listowel in July 1914. The three L&B locos carried plates on their cabsides which read, 'Lartigue Single-Rail System Mallet Patent', the latter is a reference to the French engineer who designed these special locos to run on the monorail. Engine and tender together weighed about 10 tons. Pressure in the two boilers was at 150 lbs per sq in. and the tenders could carry 200 gallons of water and 8cwt of coal. It was claimed that they could traverse a curve of 100 foot radius and haul 140 tons on the level or 40 tons up a 1 in 50 grade.** Ken Nunn collection.

Centre right: **A head on view of No.1 at Listowel which is about to take the 12.51pm train to Ballybunion on 23rd July 1914. In the very early days the locos carried an enormous headlamp which was located between the two chimneys but these seem to have been removed by the turn of the century.** Ken Nunn collection.

Bottom: **Part of the station yard at Listowel with one of the line's famous livestock wagons beside the locomotive. Stories about the need to have animals of roughly equal weight in each side of these wagons were told with great relish and no doubt were much embellished each time they were retold. An Irish MP, in the course of a filibuster at Westminster, is supposed to have told the House of Commons how a farmer, taking a cow home from market on the L&B, had to arrange for other beasts to accompany it, to balance its weight in the cattle wagon. To get these balance weights back to their rightful abodes further animals had to be found to balance them on their way back down the line. The punch line of the story was that, by the time all the beasts were back in the right place, the freight charges which the farmer had to pay were more than the value of the original cow. Whilst I am sure there is not a grain of truth in the story, this saga of cows and sheep shuttling up and down the Lartigue certainly had the potential to hold up the legislative process for quite some time.** Norman Johnston collection.

Chapter Six

THE WEST CLARE RAILWAY

THE COUNTY of Clare in the west of Ireland is surrounded by sea on three sides. In the north it borders on Galway Bay, in the south it forms the northern shore of the Shannon Estuary and in the west its coastline has to take what the mighty Atlantic throws at it. It offers some of the finest scenery and seascapes in the whole of Ireland. However, much of the county's land is poor and there are large areas of bog. Before the Great Famine of the 1840s the county was heavily populated but the failures of the potato crop, upon which so many depended for subsistence, led to Clare being most terribly affected by that disaster. The population of the county in 1841 was nearly 270,000; in 1986 it was 91,000. Much of the west of Ireland never really recovered from the Famine. The solitude and the empty roads so valued by today's tourists were bought at a terrible price nearly a century and a half ago.

The Famine with its immediate trail of death and destruction brought in its wake a wave of emigration all of which seemed to numb large parts of Ireland. The economic ramifications of the disaster killed the first bout of railway speculation in the 1840s. Only gradually did the country begin to shake off its legacy and in Clare, as in other parts of Ireland, railways began to be looked on as an engine for growth and regeneration. The first railway in the county was the Limerick & Ennis broad gauge line which opened in 1859 and was later extended in 1869 by a separate Company, the Athenry & Ennis, to make a junction with the Midland Great Western Railway's Athlone to Galway line at Athenry. At the end of the 1850s another scheme was mooted, this time in the south of the county, which had some bearing on later narrow gauge developments.

There was substantial local shipping traffic on the Shannon Estuary. On the Clare shore much of this focused on the pier at Cappagh near Kilrush. In 1858 a plan was launched for a line linking Cappagh Pier with Kilrush and Kilkee, the latter a town on the Atlantic coast with some reputation as a seaside resort. Some earthworks in connection with this proposed broad gauge line were begun but the scheme was abandoned. Various other proposals were made

but nothing became of them until 1871 when the Ennis & West Clare Railway was authorised by Parliament. This abortive scheme is of interest for two reasons: it was the first Irish narrow gauge line to be approved by Parliament, and its route from Ennis to Miltown Malbay was similar to that which was later followed by the West Clare Railway.

The Tramways Act was in the end the catalyst which brought railways to west and south Clare. The West Clare Railway was incorporated in 1884 to build a line 27 miles long from Ennis to Miltown Malbay. This was followed the same year by the South Clare Railway which was to extend the WCR line to the south west of the county with lines to Kilrush and Kilkee. Strictly speaking the two concerns were separate companies but as the SCR was in effect an extension of the WCR and was worked by the latter from the outset, the whole system is usually referred to as the WCR.

The capital of the WCR was £163,000; that of the SCR £120,000: both were underwritten by baronial guarantees. The first sod was turned on 26th January 1885 by no less a figure than Charles Stewart Parnell, the charismatic advocate of agrarian reform and home rule for Ireland, who dominated much of British and Irish politics in the 1880s. It is ironic that later, when capital to build the railway was proving hard to attract, one of the reasons given was that Parnell's campaign for home rule had affected the confidence of capitalists in the stability of the union between Britain and Ireland, and I suppose by extension, their confidence in the assurance of the continuation of their baronial guarantees. In the end a loan of £54,000 from the Board of Works averted the financial problems and allowed the line to be completed.

Though incorporated in the same year as the WCR, work on the SCR did not begin until 1890. The WCR was in a sufficiently advanced state in June 1887 for an inspection to be made by the redoubtable Major General Hutchinson who passed the line for public service. Trains began running between Ennis and Miltown Malbay on 2nd July. The first part of the SCR to open was that between Kilrush and Kilkee on 13th August 1892. The system was completed on

23rd December 1892, when following a final visit from Hutchinson, the line from Moyasta, junction of the main line from Miltown Malbay, to the Kilrush to Kilkee section, was opened for all traffic.

The WCR acquired sixteen steam locomotives over the years. The first locos were four 0-6-0Ts supplied by Bagnalls in 1887. These proved to be rather under powered and the line's reputation for indifferent time keeping may stem from these early days of operating with unsuitable locomotives. The last of the Bagnalls had been withdrawn by 1916. Ostensibly for the opening of the SCR three much more powerful locos were obtained. These were 0-6-2Ts designed by the line's Locomotive Superintendent Hopkins and built by Dübs & Co. The most unusual feature of these engines was that the coupled and trailing wheels were of the same diameter. Two of these engines lasted until the end of steam in the 1950s and one, No.5 originally named *Slieve Callan*, has been preserved. In 1894 Dübs supplied the line's first 2-6-2: this was similar to the 0-6-2Ts. Three more 2-6-2Ts were built by Green's of Leeds between 1898 and 1901 to the same basic design as the Dübs machine which became No.8 *Lisdoonvarna* The last five WCR locos were 4-6-0Ts. The first came from Kerr Stuart in 1903, the second was built by Bagnalls in 1908 whilst the last three were supplied by Hunslet, the first of these in 1912, the final pair in 1922. It is sometimes said that the two 1922 Hunslet engines were the last steam locomotives built for the Irish narrow gauge. This is not strictly speaking true. In 1928 the Clogher Valley Railway took delivery of an Atkinson Walker steam tractor, which though useless in the form it was built, had a long and active life having been acquired by the County Donegal and rebuilt to become that system's only diesel loco, No.11 *Phoenix*. In addition, as late as 1949 Bord na Mona took delivery of three well tanks from Barclay's of Kilmarnock for use on their industrial lines. I suppose it is fair to say that the 1922 Hunslet 4-6-0Ts were the last conventional steam locomotives to be supplied to an independent Irish narrow gauge company.

Services on the WCR commenced with four trains on weekdays and one on Sundays. By the summer of 1922 Bradshaw

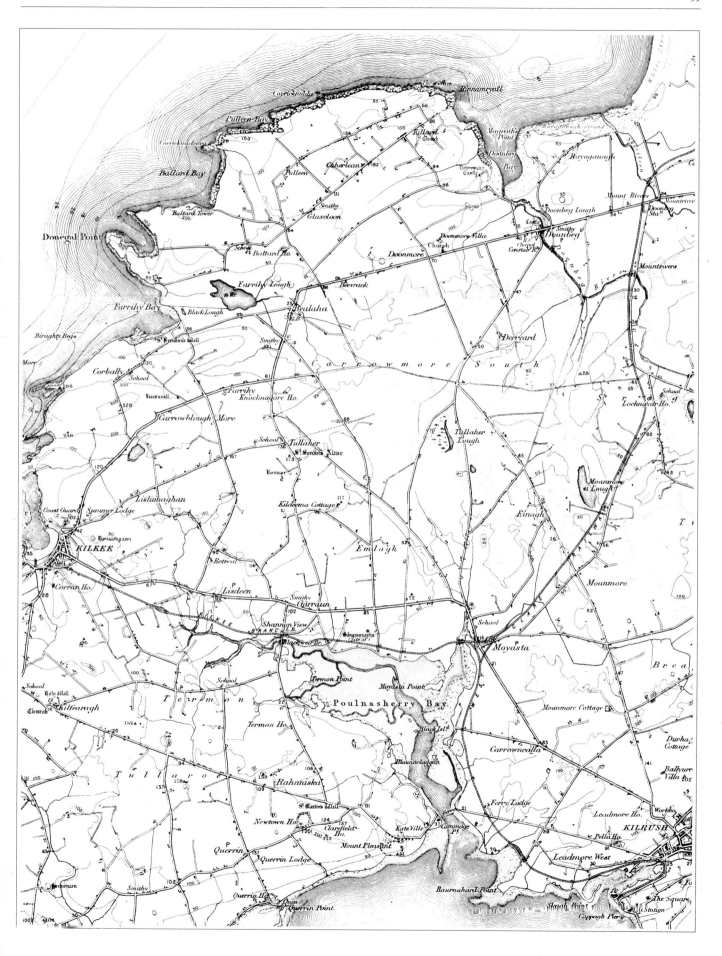

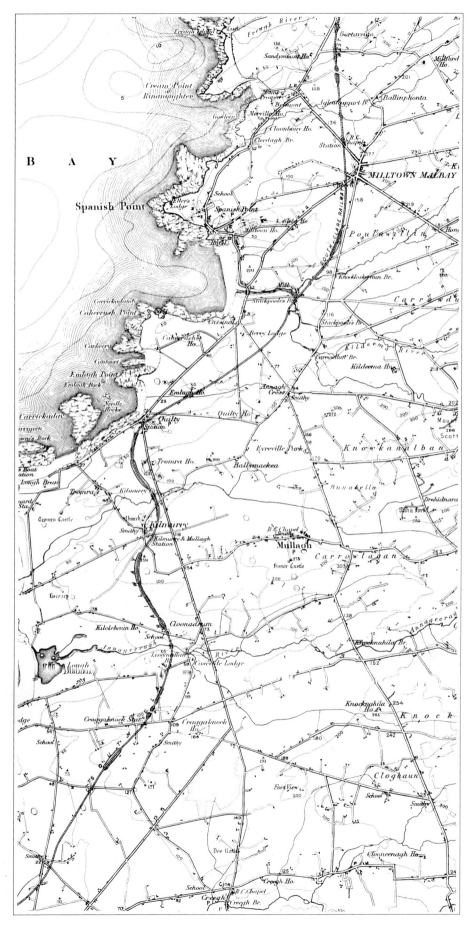

was showing that this had been reduced to two trains daily with no Sunday service. The trains ran from Ennis to Kilkee with connections to Kilrush from Moyasta Junction. This was the way the WCR was always worked with Ennis-Kilkee viewed as the main line. The poor service in 1922 may be a reflection on the 'troubles' of that year which affected the WCR badly. Moyasta Junction was the only triangular junction on the narrow gauge in the British Isles, there being a through line to enable trains to run direct from Kilrush to Kilkee. This was put in to facilitate the running of trains to meet the steamers at Cappagh Pier on the Shannon Estuary. The decline of steamer traffic on this part of the Shannon in the early years of this century diminished the significance of the through line at the junction and the branch beyond Kilrush station to the pier itself.

The WCR was a difficult line to work. there were many steep gradients on the route and the line abounded in level crossings. The Station Master at Moyasta Junction had no fewer than five of these under his control, all within a relatively short distance of the station and no published account of the line seems to be complete without the reporting of various contretemps involving trains and unopened crossing gates. Another hazard which we shall encounter again in Volume 2, on the Londonderry & Lough Swilly Railway, was wind. Part of the line south of Miltown Malbay ran very close to the Atlantic coast and trains were subject to the full rigour of Atlantic gales. Between Quilty and Kilmurry, in 1897 and again in 1899, trains were blown off the track. To deal with this, an anemometer was installed near Quilty station. Dangerous wind speeds were registered at the station by the sounding of bells linked to the anemometer. If the wind speed was over 60 mph only stock ballasted with concrete slabs was allowed to run; if the wind reached 80 mph or over the service was suspended.

It is impossible, when writing about the WCR, not to mention one of the most amusing songs ever written about a railway, which this line inspired. William Percy French was a gentler Irish contemporary of W.S.Gilbert and was famed for his songs and ballads. On one occasion he was forced to cancel a concert he was due to give in Kilkee owing to the lateness of the WCR train that was to take him there. He retaliated in the only way he knew with a comic song entitled, 'Are Ye Right There Michael Are Ye Right'. This contained such gems as:

'Kilkee! Oh, you, never get near it!

You're in luck if the train brings you back,

For the permanent way is so queer,

It spends most of its time off the track.'

Another verse has the fire going out and the passengers being encouraged by the guard to collect turf and sticks in a nearby field to get the engine going again. The Directors of the WCR were not amused and started a libel action against French. He reacted by issuing a counter claim against the railway for compensation for keeping him late for a professional engagement. Sadly, for those who enjoy courtroom frolics, someone must have warned the Directors that they were about to make fools of themselves and they dropped the case and settled out of court in the entertainer's favour.

The WCR had its fair share of woes during the 'troubles'. The area it served was a republican stronghold and clashes between the forces of the Crown and their opponents occurred regularly. The line became part of the GSR in 1925. The locos had the letter C added to their numbers and were repainted grey. That inspired choice of livery has always struck me as saying a lot about the GSR and the negative and unadventurous way it ran the railways of the Free State. During the Second World War, which in neutral southern Ireland was des-

cribed somewhat coyly as, 'the Emergency', lack of coal brought to reality the joke in 'Are Ye Right There Michael Are Ye Right'. To maintain any sort of a service the engines had to burn peat and they often travelled with a wagon of the stuff behind them, with a man throwing the fuel onto the engine's bunker as they ran. In dry weather, admittedly not that common an occurrence in the west of Ireland, sparks from the turf ignited fields of hay along the course of the line. No doubt for the purposes of compensation claims it was always the pick of the crop that got put to the torch.

When CIE took over from the GSR in the mid 1940s a report into the long term future of Ireland's railways was commissioned from Sir James Milne, the last General Manager of the English Great Western Railway. This cast doubt on the long term prospects for the WCR. Despite this in the 1950s the line embarked on a new era when complete dieselisation was decided upon. Four diesel railcars, similar to the latest CDR railcars Nos 19 and 20 which are still to be seen on the Isle of Man Railway, were bought from Walkers of Wigan. These were followed in 1955 by three Bo-Bo diesel

locomotives from the same firm to handle the line's freight traffic. Steam traction was dispensed with and the WCR became the best equipped of the surviving Irish narrow gauge lines. The old Directors of the WCR in their sepulchral boardroom had the last laugh at the shade of Percy French.

New halts were opened, services were increased, journey times were reduced as were running costs. If the Irish narrow gauge had a future this was it. In the end, dieselisation prolonged the life of the railway but did not ultimately save it. The spread of the motor car since the 1920s had been making inroads into the line's passenger traffic and the old problems of trans-shipping freight from one gauge to another were thrown into stark relief by the cheapness and directness of the motor lorry.

The end came on 31st January 1961 when the last train ran. There was much local opposition to the closure but realistically the narrow gauge had had its day and despite the gallant efforts to modernise the West Clare the economics of such a form of transport just did not make sense in the second half of the twentieth century.

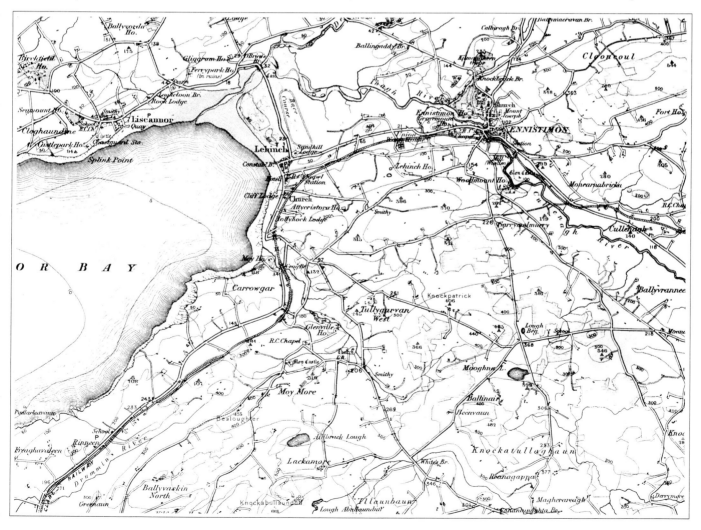

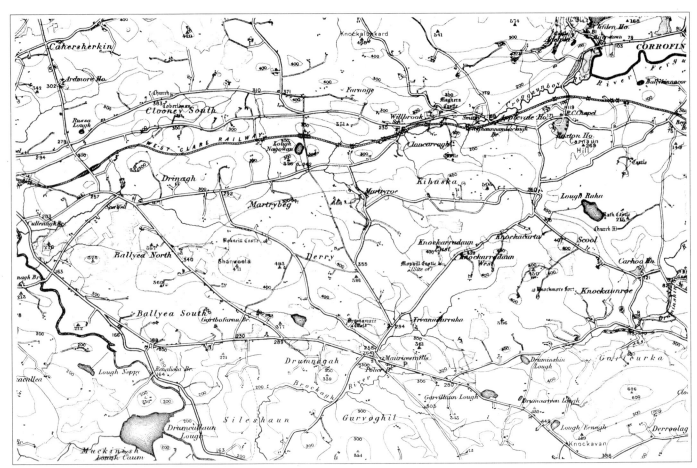

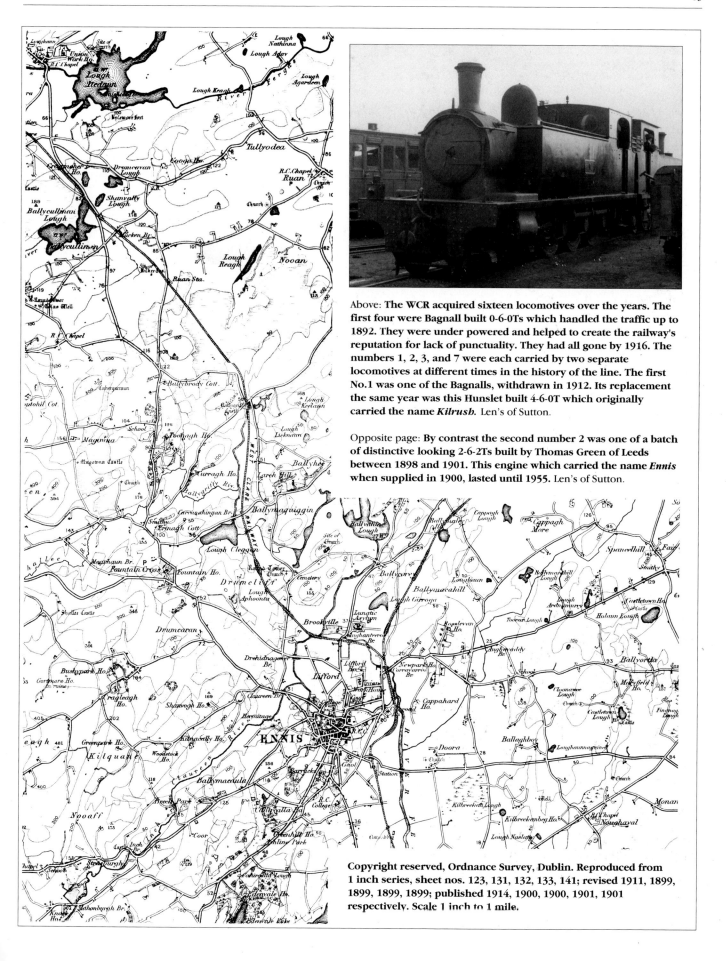

Above: The WCR acquired sixteen locomotives over the years. The first four were Bagnall built 0-6-0Ts which handled the traffic up to 1892. They were under powered and helped to create the railway's reputation for lack of punctuality. They had all gone by 1916. The numbers 1, 2, 3, and 7 were each carried by two separate locomotives at different times in the history of the line. The first No.1 was one of the Bagnalls, withdrawn in 1912. Its replacement the same year was this Hunslet built 4-6-0T which originally carried the name *Kilrush*. Len's of Sutton.

Opposite page: By contrast the second number 2 was one of a batch of distinctive looking 2-6-2Ts built by Thomas Green of Leeds between 1898 and 1901. This engine which carried the name *Ennis* when supplied in 1900, lasted until 1955. Len's of Sutton.

Copyright reserved, Ordnance Survey, Dublin. Reproduced from 1 inch series, sheet nos. 123, 131, 132, 133, 141; revised 1911, 1899, 1899, 1899, 1899; published 1914, 1900, 1900, 1901, 1901 respectively. Scale 1 inch to 1 mile.

Above: **The second No.3 was one of a pair of 4-6-0Ts supplied by Hunslet in 1922. These were the last conventional steam locomotives delivered to an Irish narrow gauge company. No.3 bore its name *Ennistimon* for only a few years before the GSR, with all the enthusiasm of a Puritan confronted with a baroque cathedral, set about dispensing with such frivolities as locomotives' names, distinctive number plates and interesting liveries and lining, to initiate the era of grey locomotives on the lines they took over. Len's of Sutton.**

Left: **No.5 is the only WCR locomotive to have survived. It is preserved on a plinth at Ennis station. In these pictures we can trace how the locomotive looked at various phases in its long career. Built in Glasgow in 1892 by Dübs and Company, one of three engines obtained at that time to work on the SCR, the engine was named *Slieve Callan*. The initials SCR can just be discerned on the number plate on the bunker in this 1920 picture of the loco at Ennis. Ken Nunn collection.**

Bottom left: **By June 1932 the original name, number and builder's plates had been removed. The only form of adornment is the GSR number plate bearing the No.5C – 'C' being the logical sectional suffix applied to the rolling stock of the GSR's Clare lines. H.C.Casserley.**

Opposite page, top: **When No.5 was photographed at Ennis on 4th July 1950 by John Edgington, it was now the property of CIE. The GSR number plate has now been replaced by a plain painted number in a style similar to that used on the company's broad gauge locos. In all three pictures the engine retains the wooden shutters used to keep some of the force of the fierce gales experienced at times in the west of Ireland, out of the loco's cab.**

Above left: **In the course of 1922 the WCR had at different times, two No.7s of totally different designs. They began the year with *Lady Inchiquin,* a 0-6-2T. When that was withdrawn the replacement engine, also numbered 7, was a new Hunslet built 4-6-0T. The second No.7 was given the name *Malbay,* and had the dubious distinction, by dint of a later works number than her sister No.3 *Ennistimon,* of being the last conventional new steam locomotive to be built for the Irish narrow gauge. Len's of Sutton.**

Right: ***Slieve Callan's* two sisters are depicted here. No.6, originally named *Saint Senan,* was not withdrawn until 1956. She is seen leaving Ennis on a mixed train on 30th June 1938. H.C.Casserley.**

Above right: **The other 1892 built Dübs 0-6-2T was the first No.7 *Lady Inchiquin.* She was only six years old, and the goods shed at Ennis had not yet been completed, when she was photographed there on 15th September 1898. It is strange how some engines in a class outlive others. When withdrawn in 1922 *Lady Inchiquin* had served the railway for a respectable 30 years yet her two sisters lasted over 60 years. Ken Nunn collection.**

Left: **Sister engines of the Thomas Green built No.2** *Ennis,* **which we saw on page 62, were No.4** *Liscannor* **and No.9** *Fergus.* **No.4, built in 1901, had an inexplicably short innings, being withdrawn in 1928. No.9, seen here in GSR days at Kilrush, dated from 1898 and lasted until the end of steam in the 1950s. These 2-6-2Ts were almost identical to an earlier engine built by Dübs in 1894 which in turn was an enlarged version of the Dübs 0-6-2Ts, seen on the previous page.** Len's of Sutton.

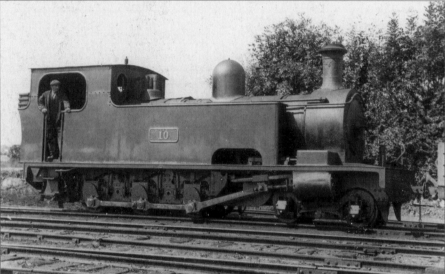

Centre left and below: **No.10 was the WCR's first 4-6-0T. It was later joined by another four locomotives of this wheel arrangement. Built by Kerr Stuart in 1903 and named** *Lahinch,* **she was designed by the WCR Locomotive Engineer W.J.Carter, and had the highest tractive effort of all the engines on the line. No.10 is pictured both on her native heath, and on the mixed gauge track at the GSR's Inchicore works in Dublin.** Both Len's of Sutton.

Bottom: **The second 4-6-0T to be delivered was numbered 11, and is seen here at the place after which it was named,** *Kilkee.* **Built by Bagnalls in 1909, No.11 lasted until 1953.** H.C.Casserley.

Top: **This little four wheel inspection car originated on the T&D. It was used on several of the GSR's narrow gauge lines, being transported from one to the other on a broad gauge wagon. This Ford engined vehicle spent its last decade on the WCR and was photographed at Ennis in July 1950.** John Edgington.

Above left: **A simple flat wagon is used to convey a piece of agricultural machinery. Agriculture is, was and always will be, Ireland's principal economic activity.** D.G.Coakham.

Above right: **6-wheel brake No.17C was photographed at Ennis in June 1961 after services on the line had ended.** John Edgington.

Left: **Coach No.33C was one of several splendid 6-wheel saloons with large picture windows which were originally First class only and were built to cater for the line's tourist traffic. As built they had rather ornate stained glass in the windows on the clerestory roof and in the quarterlights. The stained glass had been painted over and the coaches had been relegated to Thirds only and indeed virtually made redundant by the coming of diesel railcars when they were photographed at Ennis in 1955. Despite this they still retain traces of their *fin de siecle* elegance.** H.C.Casserley.

Centre, far left: **A rather different style of coach building is evidenced by No.47C. This was one of a number of trailers fabricated at Inchicore to run with the railcars. Not much sign of clerestories or stained glass here in this strictly utilitarian vehicle which owes much to 1950s bus design for its inspiration.** H.C.Casserley.

Left: **This two-plank open wagon, into which coal is being transferred from the broad gauge wagon on the adjacent track, at Ennis in 1934, still faintly bears the initials WCR on its sides.** H.C.Casserley.

Below: **The WCR trains shared the broad gauge station at Ennis. No.292, an E2 class 0-4-4T has arrived with the 3.30pm from Limerick to Ennis whilst 0-6-2T No.5 is about to depart with the connecting 4.55pm to Kilrush on 4th July 1950. Normally, but not in this instance, trains from Ennis ran through to Kilkee with a connecting service to Kilrush being provided at Moyasta Junction. The mixed narrow gauge train is made up of two of the former First class saloons, an ordinary coach and a variety of wagons.** John Edgington.

Right: **In GSR days 4-6-0T No.3 takes water at Ennis.** Len's of Sutton.

Below: **On 31st May 1924 2-6-2T No.2 *Ennis* is shunting at the station whose name it bears.** Ken Nunn collection.

Below, centre: **On the same day the 4.30pm mixed train to Kilkee leaves Ennis headed by 4-6-0T No.1 *Kilrush*.** Ken Nunn collection.

Below, centre right: **For the first 1¼ miles out of Ennis, broad and narrow gauge tracks ran parallel to each other, crossing the River *Fergus* on separate bridges. On 8th June 1932 2-6-2T No.9 is approaching Ennis along this stretch of track with a freight train.** H.C.Casserley.

Bottom: **No.7C heads a mixed train out of Ennis in the 1930s. The angle of the camera makes the 5ft 3in gauge tracks in the foreground really look broad gauge.** Len's of Sutton.

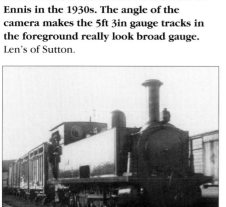

Top: **The WCR's workshops and main loco shed were at Ennis. The company's initials can be seen on the decorative plinth on top of the workshop building.** H.C.Casserley.

Above: **The loco shed was to the right of the repair shops and was another wooden structure. No.5C is outside the shed on 5th June 1932.** H.C.Casserley.

Above: **Was wood an appropriate material for the construction of an engine shed? It certainly looked a bit the worse for wear in this late 1930s picture with No.9 in attendance.** Len's of Sutton.

Left: **Moyasta Junction 43 miles from Ennis was the spot where the lines to Kilkee and Kilrush diverged. No.3 takes water before working a short train to Kilrush.** Len's of Sutton.

Opposite page: **Lahinch, 21 miles out from Ennis, was where the line met the coast for the first time. This was a popular seaside resort which many excursionists visited every year by means of the railway. These 1930s views of trains at Lahinch show No.1 on a train for Ennis** (courtesy *Railway Magazine*) **and a southbound train at the other platform. A turntable was installed in the 1950s to enable the railcars to turn here on workings from Ennis.** Len's of Sutton.

Left and below: **Kilkee, 45 miles from Ennis, was another seaside town popular with visitors and trippers. The contrast between the normal two coach service train in charge of No.10, (Len's of Sutton) and the lengthy Sunday excursion headed by No.11C on 15th July 1934, is a reflection of how important this sort of traffic was for the railway.** H.C.Casserley.

Bottom left: **Kilkee on a wet May day in 1956. By this time normal steam services had come to an end but No.5 had been repainted in an ornate fictitious livery for use in the making of a feature film entitled 'Three Leaves of a Shamrock', part of which was filmed on the West Clare.** *Slieve Callan*'s career in the movies enabled her to outlive her sisters and ultimately to find her way into preservation. Walter McGrath.

Photographs on the opposite page:

Top left: **Kilrush was 47 miles from Ennis. No.2 heads a short train towards the station in June 1953.** J.H.Price.

Top right: **On 5th July 1953 No.2 was again at Kilrush, this time shunting wagons at the station's goods yard.** Courtesy *Railway Magazine*.

Bottom: **The ubiquitous No.5 is ready to leave Kilrush with the 8.00am to Ennis on 5th July 1950. The tracks seen heading off from the rear of the train continued for a mile or so to Cappagh Pier. The line to the pier had fallen into disuse as early as the 1920s.** John Edgington.

Photographs on the opposite page:

Top left: **The coming of the railcars and later of the three diesel locos transformed the WCR and gave it a fighting chance of survival. Shortly after their arrival one of the railcars was photographed at Kilkee in the summer of 1952.** Walter McGrath.

Top right: **With only a few months left to the West Clare before closure, railcar No.3389 forms a Kilkee train at the junction on 22nd September 1960.** Walter McGrath.

Centre left: **On 24th June 1959 the connecting service from Kilrush had arrived at Moyasta Junction and passengers are moving across to join the railcar from Kilkee, which will form the through service to Ennis, that has just arrived at the other platform.** D.G.Coakham.

Centre right: **The loop at Moyasta Junction, originally built to enable trains connecting with the steamers on the Shannon estuary at Cappagh Pier, to run through to Kilkee, once again had a regular passenger service**

in the diesel era. **Some railcars ran over the loop, to provide a through service from Kilrush to Kilkee, as was the case in this instance, on 12th July 1957.** D.G.Coakham.

Bottom: **The diesel locos were equally at home on passenger trains when required. They were used to haul railcar trailers or in this instance a coach which had been in service on the Cavan & Leitrim until its closure in 1959. The coach was taken to Inchicore and was totally refurbished for just one year's work on the West Clare. F502 was on this passenger duty on 22nd September 1960.** Walter McGrath.

Photographs on this page:

Top: **On a return service later that day, F502 pauses at the station described by Percy French in his famous ballad as, 'sweet Corofin'. In his book** *'Rails in the Isle of Man: A Colour Celebration'* **(Midland Publishing, 1993), Robert Hendry relates how the General manager of the Isle of Man Railway tried to buy one of these locos from CIE when the WCR closed down but**

could not get them to accept a realistic price. What a shame that one of these locos did not join the County Donegal railcars Nos 19 and 20, the models for the Walker railcars used to modernise the WCR, on that wonderful 3ft gauge sanctuary in the middle of the Irish Sea. Walter McGrath.

Above: **On 18th July 1960, a special organised by the Farnborough Railway Club was probably the last passenger train ever to traverse the section from Kilrush out to Cappagh Pier. One of the diesels and a van gingerly venture along this rarely used part of the WCR on that occasion.** J.W.C.Caley, courtesy of Walter McGrath.

Top: **The modernisation of the narrow gauge in Clare was completed in 1955 with the delivery of three centre cab Bo-Bo diesel locomotives from Walkers of Wigan, who had built the railcars. The power bogies of the locos and the railcars were interchangeable. With the arrival of the diesel locos steam haulage on the line's freight services was dispensed with. After the line closed in June 1961, F503 was photographed at Ennis by John Edgington.**

I have included this picture for two reasons. First, the loco stands on a most interesting piece of track where a 5ft 3in line crosses over two 3ft gauge lines. Also of considerable interest is the gentleman with the camera who is to the right of the locomotive. This is Henry Casserley, who sadly died in 1991; his superb pictures of the Irish narrow gauge, taken since the 1920s, grace many of the pages in this book, and its companion volume. Those of

us with an interest in the railways of Ireland owe him an immense debt of gratitude for his work in recording them over many decades.

Above: **If the Irish narrow gauge had a future this was it. F502 pauses with the goods at Lahinch to allow a passenger train to overtake it. This picture was taken on 12th June 1957.** D.G.Coakham.

Right: **In the last summer of the WCR, railcar No.3387 hauling a trailer pauses at Corofin with a train for Ennis.** Courtesy *Railway Magazine.*

Below: **An Ennistimon F501 heads a Kilkee bound train. The first vehicle is the rebuilt C&L coach, the second is one of the Inchicore built railcar trailers.** Courtesy *Railway Magazine.*

Chapter Seven

THE CAVAN & LEITRIM RAILWAY

THE COUNTY of Leitrim in the province of Connaught is one of the most thinly populated in Ireland. It is an area of poor land, small farms and little industrial activity. Leitrim is a land of lakes and streams and though a delight to tourists, especially those given to cruising on inland waterways, it was not the most promising place to contemplate building railways in the last century.

The first line in the area was that of the MGWR from Longford to Sligo which opened in 1862. Dromod, on this line, was to be the southern terminus of the Cavan & Leitrim Railway. Away to the north east in 1885 construction began on a branch of the GNR from Ballyhaise, on the line from Clones to Cavan, to Belturbet in County Cavan. This was the northern terminus of

the Cavan & Leitrim Railway main line.

To open up south Leitrim, in December 1883 the Cavan, Leitrim and Roscommon Light Railway and Tramway Company was set up. Incorporated under the Tramways Act, it sought baronial guarantees on its capital. The original plan was for a line from Dromod to Belturbet with a branch from Ballinamore through Arigna to Boyle in County Roscommon, hence the inclusion of that county's name in the company's title. In 1884 the Grand Jury of Roscommon refused to have anything to do with the scheme and the extension beyond Arigna was dropped. The other two counties shouldered the burden of their guarantees and work began in the Autumn of 1885 on the Dromod to Belturbet section. Construction of the branch to Arigna, which was

always referred to as the tramway, began in 1886. The Arigna line was built to tap the potential traffic from the deposits of coal and iron ore found there. It was one of the few places in Ireland where these amoeba of heavy industrialisation were to be found together. Nothing much ever came of the iron but Arigna coal kept the C&L afloat for many decades.

The main line was ready by the summer of 1887. It was inspected and approved by the ubiquitous Major General Hutchinson in October of that year. Though traffic was substantial it did not live up to the very optimistic forecasts of the line's promoters and the first operating surplus was not recorded until 1893. All through the C&L's independent existence profits were never sufficient to pay the guaranteed interest and the

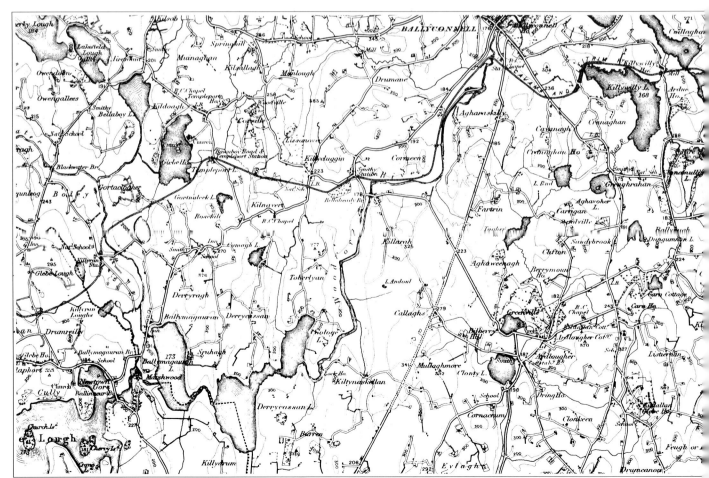

ratepayers were called upon to make up the difference.

The Grand Jury had the right to have directors on the board of the railway to safeguard the interests of the ratepayers who were underwriting the line. In the years following 1898, when the Grand Juries were replaced by County Councils in Ireland, the history of the C&L was clouded by acrimonious disputes between directors representing the shareholders and those from the County Council. Other Irish narrow gauge lines had the same mix of shareholders and ratepayers representatives but nowhere else did relations between the two groups sour and fester as on the C&L. There were two camps in the boardroom and political and religious rivalries and prejudices exacerbated the discord. The Grand Jury directors had been generally landowners and were, if readers will excuse a lapse into neo-Marxist jargon, of the same class as the shareholders' directors. The new County Councils were much more democratic and in order to thwart their influence, in 1902 the C&L establishment rigged the composition of the board, to ensure that the shareholders' directors would always have a majority over those representing the ratepayers. The attitude towards the County Council appointees seems to have

been one of shut up and pay up.

One constant source of dispute was the relationship between the C&L and the Arigna Mining Company which had been set up in 1888. The two concerns had a number of directors in common and the argument was frequently aired that the C&L directors spent more time and effort involved with the affairs of the mining company than with the railway. It was also implied that as the dividends of the C&L were guaranteed by the ratepayers the directors took less interest in it for this reason. There was a quite spectacular row in 1906 which resulted in the loss of a grant of £24,000 of government money to build an extension up to the coal mines from the existing terminus at Arigna.

In 1895 the word Roscommon was dropped from the title of the C&L reflecting the failure to extend the tramway beyond Arigna into that county. However in the two decades following the opening of the railway some fascinating and some fanciful schemes for the extension of the system were mooted, which if they had been successful, would have created a narrow gauge empire, of which the C&L would have been an important part. In the 1880s plans were promoted for a variety of tramways one of which would have penetrated as far south as Woodlawn on the MGWR Athlone to

Galway line. In 1889 the C&L had discussions with the Clogher Valley Railway on a plan to link the two lines. This scheme was revived in 1900 when the Ulster & Connaught Light Railway Act was passed. The C&L in the end opposed this grandiose plan which would have produced another epic for the narrow gauge masochist to rival that from Londonderry to Burtonport. In 1896, perhaps influenced by the possibility of government funding under the Railway Act of that year, a scheme was mooted for an extension of the Arigna line northwards to Collooney in County Sligo. If this one had come off it could have provided this tiny village with its fourth railway station. Away from these great strategic lines the most obvious and much needed extension of the C&L was that of the Arigna tramway up to the mines it was supposed to serve. The line terminated several miles from the mines and despite the logic of having an extension built, it took over thirty years and indirectly, a world war, to achieve it.

The boardroom rows of 1906 led to the loss of the Government funding for the line on offer at that time. Another scheme floundered in 1914. The need to maximise Irish coal production during the Great War was the catalyst which led to the construction of the 4 mile 374 yard extension of the

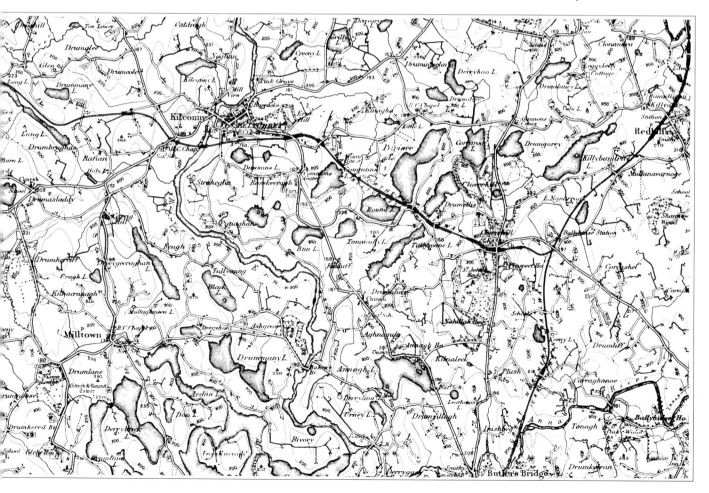

The extension to the mines at Arigna had not been built when this map was revised.

tramway in the end. The Irish Railway Executive Committee, which ran the country's railways during the war, provided the £60,000 needed for the work which began in the autumn of 1918 and was completed in 1920. Part of the route followed that of a wagonway built in the 1830s. One of the pits served by the new line, that at Aughabehy, was exhausted by 1930, but the pit at Derreenavoggy kept the C&L in business for the next four decades.

The locomotive history of the independent C&L was one of the most straightforward of any of the Irish narrow gauge lines though it became more complex under the ownership of the GSR and CIE. For the opening of the system eight 4-4-0Ts were ordered from Robert Stephenson and Company of Newcastle-upon-Tyne. Four of these had skirts and condensing gear for working the tramway. The tramway quartet had parts of their cab backplates cut away to improve the driver's view and a duplicate set of driving gear at the back of the cab to enable him to drive the engine whilst keeping a constant lookout. The 4-4-0Ts were named after the daughters of directors of the C&L except for No.8 which bore the

name *Queen Victoria.* Four of these first engines lasted until the line's closure.

One problem encountered with these engines in the early years of the line was that, on the tramway, where to comply with Board of Trade regulations, they had to run cab first, the leading coupled wheels tended to damage the track. To overcome this the C&L decided to run the engines chimney first but in doing so they fell foul of the Board of Trade. The Board insisted in 1893 that, if they were to run this way, the driver still had to be at the front. To comply with this, Nos 7 and 8, the regular tramway engines, were fitted with a brake, regulator and reversing lever in front of the smokebox. No cab was fitted at the front to protect the driver, so pity the poor C&L drivers, standing on the front of their engines, hanging on to their controls as they bounced and jolted their way to Arigna, exposed to the full rigour of the Irish weather. It seems that by 1898 these regulations were either relaxed or were being ignored and that this lunacy was dispensed with. The controls were soon removed from the fronts of the engines concerned.

The only other locomotive purchased by

the C&L turned out to be something of a white elephant. In 1904 Robert Stephenson designed and built No.9 *King Edward*. This 0-6-4T was much larger and more powerful than the 4-4-0s. It was also much heavier and despite the fact that it had flangeless centre drivers, it played havoc with the permanent way. It was barred from the tramway and it was decreed that it should only run bunker first on the main line. Even when it ran in reverse it still managed to spread the track because of its long wheel base. The directors admitted defeat and only allowed No.9 to be used in emergencies. It was offered for sale in 1922 but found no takers. The engine was eventually removed for scrapping in 1934.

The first foreign engines to run on the C&L were two from the Northern Counties Committee's narrow gauge lines in County Antrim, which were moved to Ballinamore at the behest of the wartime Railway Executive to assist in the construction and operation of the extension to the mines at Arigna. These had been among the first 3ft gauge engines to run in Ireland, having been built by Black Hawthorn for the Ballymena, Cushendall & Red Bay Railway

in the mid 1870s. These two 0-4-2T engines, numbered 101A and 102A, stayed on the C&L from April 1920 until November 1921.

After the interlude with the two NCC locomotives, the original C&L 4-4-0Ts soldiered on, working the line until 1934 when the GSR dispatched the four 2-4-2Ts, which had made up the entire fleet of the CB&P section, which had been closed in 1932, to Ballinamore. They were renumbered 10L-13L. On the face of it, these engines, with their large driving wheels designed to give a decent turn of speed on the CB&P suburban services into Cork, were a strange choice for the C&L. Although they were banned from the tramway and one of them, No.11L, was scrapped in 1939, they proved themselves to be useful engines on the main line. The remaining three lasted until the 1950s. No.13L was withdrawn in 1954 but Nos 10L and 12L lasted to the end of services on the line.

The last four additions to the C&L fleet were all transfers from the Tralee & Dingle line in County Kerry, though they were not renumbered. The first arrived in 1941. Nos 3T and 4T were 2-6-0Ts. No.3T was built by Hunslet in 1889. The other engine came

from Kerr, Stuart and Company in 1903. In 1949 the next emigrant from Kerry arrived in the form of No.5T, a Hunslet built 2-6-2T of 1892. This engine did a lot of work on the C&L, especially on the coal trains. On the closure of the C&L it was purchased for preservation in the USA from where it has recently been repatriated and put to work on a section of its old line in Kerry which was reopened in 1992 *(see page 108)*. The final T&D machine came late in the day. This was No.6T, another Hunslet 2-6-0T, very similar to No.3T. On the closure of the T&D in 1953 it had first been moved to the West Clare to work on that line's goods trains. It was made redundant by the purchase of three Walker diesel locomotives in 1955 and was sent to Inchicore to await its fate. The upsurge of coal traffic on the C&L in the mid 50s earned it a reprieve and it was sent to Ballinamore in 1957 and was in use up to closure.

Part of the great attraction for railway enthusiasts of the C&L was that it was steam worked throughout the whole of its existence. The line from Dromod to Belturbet was worked as one section with connections to Arigna being provided at

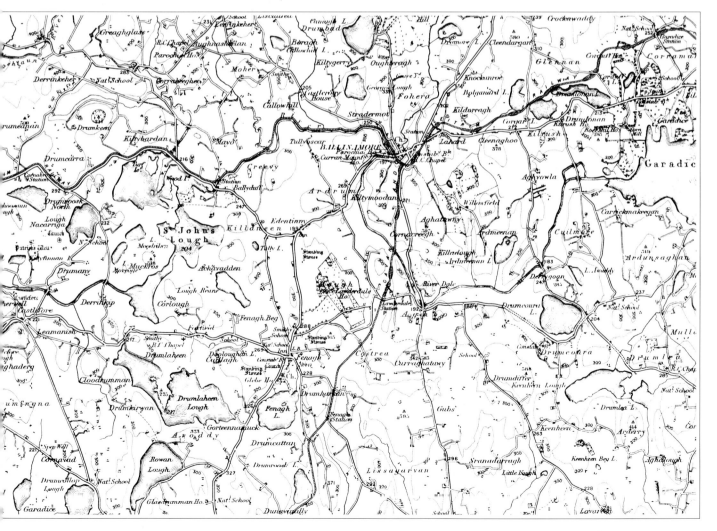

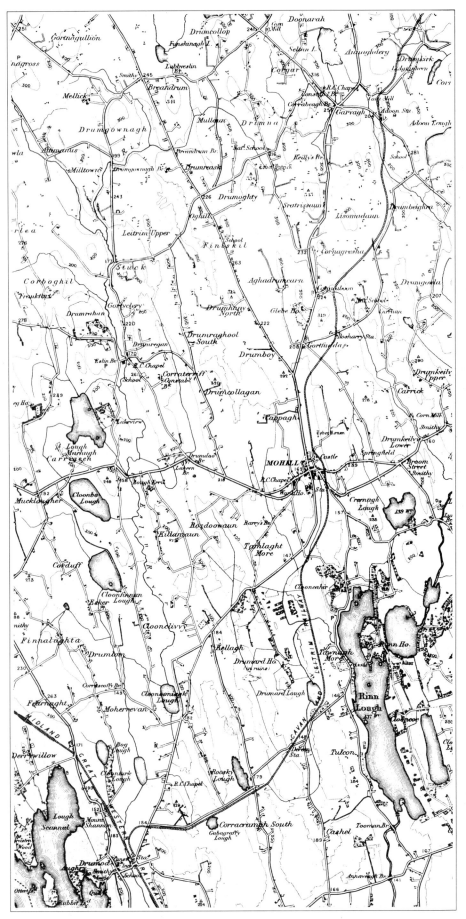

Ballinamore. There were engine sheds at Dromod and Belturbet but the line's focal point was Ballinamore where most of the engines were kept and the workshops were located. Up to 1930 all the major repairs to locomotives were carried out at Ballinamore. The last engine to be out-shopped there was No.1 *Isabel*. The works were subsequently run down and engines due for heavy repairs were sent to Inchicore.

C&L trains were generally mixed. When the railway opened, three trains each way were offered on the main line with connections to Arigna from Ballinamore. By the 1950s this had declined to three Ballinamore to Dromod workings to connect with broad gauge trains on the Dublin to Sligo line. One of these workings was extended to and from Belturbet to provide a service on that section and there was also one train each day to Arigna and back. There was never a passenger service beyond Arigna on the extension up to the mines. By the 1940s and 1950s it was the coal traffic which kept the line going. Up to six coal trains daily operated to and from Arigna during the Second World War. Arigna coal may not have been of the highest quality but it was extremely welcome in southern Ireland during the war when imported coal was very hard to come by. In the 1950s the main customers for Arigna coal were the cement factories at Limerick and Drogheda. Incredible as it sounds in this day and age, the handling of the coal was never mechanised and at Belturbet it had to be shovelled by hand from the narrow gauge trains into broad gauge wagons.

By 1958 the coal traffic had slackened somewhat and it was estimated that the line was losing some £40,000 per year. The final blow was the announcement, by the Irish Government, of plans to build a new coal fired power station on the shores of Lough Allen near Arigna which would absorb the output of the mines. The last trains ran on 31st March 1959. Services on that sad day were worked by the T&D engines but one of the original 1887 4-4-0Ts, No.4, was in steam as the standby engine. The C&L certainly got value for money from its original locomotives. Fittingly, two of them survived the cutters torch; No.2 *Kathleen* is in the care of the Ulster Folk and Transport Museum and No.3 *Lady Edith* has been preserved in the USA.

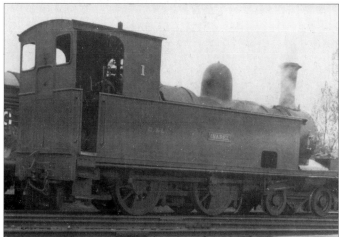

Above left: **The original nine C&L locos were still in existence when the GSR took over in 1925. Two of these were quickly scrapped, No.5 *Gertrude* in 1925 and No.6 *May* in 1927. In the days when the line was independent, the livery used on locos was lined green. The lining on the ends of the tanks can clearly be seen in this head-on view of No.8 *Queen Victoria*, taken at Ballinamore in May 1920.** Ken Nunn collection.

Above and left: **Some C&L engines retained their name plates and brass cabside numerals well into the GSR period. No.1 *Isabel* (left) displays these at Ballinamore in June 1932, as does No.4 *Violet* (above).** H.C.Casserley.

Below: **In 1934 No.7 *Olive* became the first engine to go to Inchicore for overhaul. She returned without her nameplate and the brass numeral on her cabside. A small metal plate bearing the number 7L, – 'L' being the GSR section letter for the line, was affixed in their stead.** Len's of Sutton.

Above: **No.7 was scrapped in 1945 and No.1 followed in 1949 but four of the original eight engines lasted until the line closed in 1959. No.4 was in steam at Ballinamore in July 1950. Now in its seventh decade, CIE had become the loco's third owner in the course of its long career which still had some years to run.** John Edgington.

Far left: **Engines were taken to and from Inchicore on broad gauge well wagons. No.2 was photographed there in July 1950. This engine was subsequently saved for preservation in Belfast Transport Museum.** John Edgington.

Centre left: **The C&L's other loco, the not very successful No.9** *King Edward,* **is seen here. It apparently was rarely steamed from about 1920 on. The wisp of steam from its safety valves shows that it was in use on 17th May 1924.** Ken Nunn collection.

Left: **No.9 lies out of use at Ballinamore in the late 1920s. It is in quite good external condition with a lot of its lining visible.** Len's of Sutton.

To supplement the C&L's stock of engines, which by 1934 was down to the six remaining 4-4-0TS, the GSR had the four 2-4-2Ts from the closed CB&P overhauled and sent north. They arrived at Dromod in August and September 1934. On the face of it, they were unlikely engines for the C&L with their 4ft 6in driving wheels and their reputation for swiftness. One was tried on the Arigna tramway and actually got stuck on one of the severe curves on the extension to the mines. After that embarrassment they never ventured up the tramway again but they gave good service on the main line. The former CB&P Nos 4, 5, 6 and 7 became 10L to 13L on the C&L. No.11L was withdrawn in 1939, No.13L lasted until 1954; the other two remained in use up to closure.

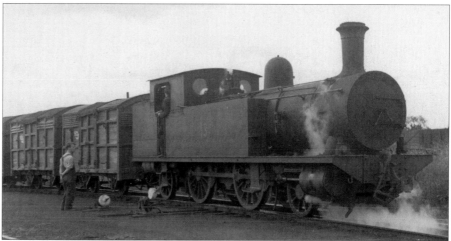

Top: **On 1st July 1950, No.12L heads the 3.10pm train from Ballinamore to Dromod at the former location. Most of the train consists of wagons of Arigna coal.** John Edgington.

Centre right: **No.13L makes up a train at Dromod the same day. For many years this engine was based here.** John Edgington.

Right: **No.10L just about fits onto the turntable at Ballinamore. This loco retained its GSR cast numberplate until withdrawal.** H.C.Casserley.

Left: **Some of the refugees from the T&D which found sanctuary on the C&L are featured here. No.5, the T&D's unique 2-6-2T came to Ballinamore after a visit to Inchicore, in 1949. She proved a very popular engine and was in constant use for the next decade. She was photographed in the yard at Ballinamore on 26th May 1958.** John Edgington.

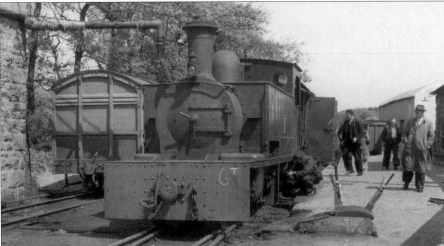

Centre left: **The final T&D engine arrived as late as 1957. No.6 had first gone to the West Clare following the closure of its own line. Made redundant there by the arrival of the three diesel locos, it was sent to Inchicore to await its fate but an upsurge in coal traffic on the C&L in the late 1950s led to it being sent to Ballinamore. Built in 1898 by Hunslet, this engine was very similar to No.3. Like the other Kerry engines it was not renumbered. It carried 6T plates on its tanks. No.6T is here seen taking water at Drumshambo on a train to Arigna on 26th May 1958.** John Edgington.

Opposite page, top: **The arrival of these engines from other closed 3ft gauge lines led to a much greater variety of motive power on the C&L in its last decade. This could be seen to good effect at Ballinamore where the C&L's main shed and repair shops were located. Outside the shed on 26th May 1958 are from left to right: 2-4-2T No.12, ex T&D No.3 and an unidentified C&L 4-4-0T. Another of the CB&P engines is shunting in the distance to the left of the picture.** John Edgington.

Opposite page, bottom: **Later in the day the line up had changed with 4-4-0T No.4 and the T&D 2-6-0T No.3 in the foreground.** John Edgington.

Above: **The first Kerry engines to come north were the 2-6-0Ts Nos.3 and 4 which arrived in 1941. No.4, a Kerr Stuart engine, was not much used perhaps on account of alleged weak brakes. By contrast, judging from the photographic record, No.3 seems to have been a very busy engine indeed. She was delivered in 1891 and was used in the work of constructing the Tralee & Dingle line. It is ironic that its last work was put in on the trains used to demolish the C&L. No.3 is coming off shed in this early 1950s view.** John Edgington.

Opposite page, top: **On 27th April 1956, 2-6-2T No.5 is raising steam whilst the two 4-4-0Ts in the foreground, Nos.8 and 3, were not in use that day.** There are some interesting differences between the two C&L locos. The top corners of No.8's cab backplate have been cut away. This is a relic of the very early days of the line when this was one of the engines designated to work on the tramway. The cutaway cab backplate was to improve the crew's vision when she was running with the cab leading. No.8 also retains her original style of chimney and dome whereas No.3 sports the short GSR chimney and a dome, believed to have come from one of the West Clare's Hunslet

4-6-0Ts. Both of these adornments had been acquired by No.3 on visits to Inchicore. John Edgington.

Opposite page, bottom: **Our travels along the C&L begin at Dromod, the southern terminus. On 7th June 1932 No.7 *Isabel*, still with her nameplate in place, is at the head of the 10.21am to Belturbet.** H.C.Casserley.

Below left: **4-4-0T No.4 has just been turned at Dromod on 2nd April 1956.** Oddly, for a line situated in a part of Ireland abounding in rivers and lakes, the C&L had problems with its water supply. Some engines were fitted with a valve from which steam could

be extracted, to operate the pulsometer used to fill the water tank beside the single road shed at Dromod. W.A.C.Smith.

Below right: **Mohill, 5 miles out from Dromod, was the first station of significance encountered heading north on the C&L main line. On 27th May 1950, 10L, the 2-4-2T with the cast numberplate, heads out of the station with a train for Dromod.** H.C.Casserley.

Bottom: **2-4-2T No.12L takes water at Mohill on 1st July 1950. The train is the 3.10pm from Ballinamore to Mohill.** John Edgington.

Above: **Ballinamore was the hub of the railway and it changed very little over the years. No.7 *Olive* is shunting at the south end of the station in June 1932. This engine was sent to Inchicore in 1939 where it became a source of spare parts to keep its sisters running. It was finally scrapped in 1945.** H.C.Casserley.

Below: **Since the arrival of this loco from the T&D in 1941 the C&L had two No.3s. The Kerry No.3 stands beside one of the ground frames used to control the points and signals at Ballinamore. The C&L did not go in for such effete luxuries as signal boxes.** Len's of Sutton.

Above: **Ballinamore, perhaps in deference to its status as the line's headquarters, possessed the only station footbridge on the railway. This proved a great asset for photographers. In this case it was John Edgington who was using it to good effect to record the 4.30pm Belturbet to Dromod arriving at the station on 25th May 1958.**

Below: **On 25th May 1958 No.10L brings the short 12.20pm Dromod to Belturbet train into Ballinamore. A contrast in coaching stock is apparent. Brake composite No.5 is in the Arigna branch bay whilst the mainline train has No.7, the coach which was given a bus type body at Inchicore in 1953, on its original C&L frame.**
John Edgington.

Above: **Ballyconnell was 11 miles from Ballinamore and 6 from Belturbet. In April 1956 the 12.20 from Dromod to Belturbet, the only through working along the whole length of the line by this stage, was recorded at Ballyconnell by two different photographers on two separate occasions. On April 2nd, 4-4-0T No.4 was in charge of the train,** W.A.C.Smith.

Left: **On April 27th 2-4-2T No.10L was the loco. On both days the make up of the train was remarkably similar with cattle wagons predominating.** John Edgington.

Below: **At Belturbet the C&L made a connection with the GNR broad gauge branch from Ballyhaise on the Clones to Cavan Town line. Conveniently, C&L and GNR trains used opposite sides of the same platform. Trains on Ireland's two gauges are apparent in this picture dating from April 1948. The C&L train is headed by 4-4-0T No.2. This loco which had in former days been named *Kathleen* was acquired for preservation in Belfast Transport Museum when the railway closed. The only passenger in sight can be named; he is a young Richard Casserley, which gives away the identity of the photographer!**

Top: **On 4th May 1957, GNR P class 4-4-0 No.27, one of a number of its type with 6ft 6in driving wheels, rests between turns, as the narrow gauge engine No12L shunts a wagon.** D.G.Coakham

Right: **This trans-shipment shed and platform at Belturbet provided a convenient method of transferring goods from one gauge to another.** John Edgington.

Bottom right: **No.10L takes water amidst the remains of the C&L engine shed at Belturbet on 27th April 1950.** John Edgington.

Below: **No.10L leaves Belturbet with the 4.20pm departure for Dromod on 27th April 1950.** John Edgington.

Top: **The former CB&P engines performed sterling service on the C&L main line. Here No.13L heads the 12.00pm Dromod to Belturbet train on 1st July 1950.** John Edgington.

Above: **Towards the end, the engines on the C&L were allowed to deteriorate into a dreadful external condition. No10L has a rather battered smokebox door and the**

paint has been burnt off her chimney, as she waits, under Ballinamore's famous footbridge, to restart the 4.30pm Belturbet to Dromod on 20th May 1958. **John Edgington.**

Opposite page, top: **The bay at the south end of Ballinamore's main platform was the usual starting point for Arigna trains. The C&L's two No.3s are seen in the bay**

some five years apart. C&L 4-4-0T No.3 waits for the off on 17th May 1950. H.C.Casserley.

Opposite page, bottom: **The other No.3, the ex-T&D 2-6-0T, is at the head of the 1.50pm to Arigna on 19th April 1955. The Arigna train is composed of the usual brake composite carriage and a rake of empty coal wagons.** H.C.Casserley.

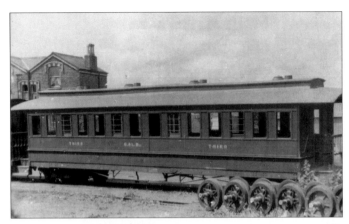
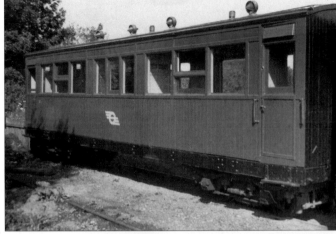

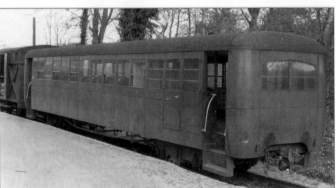

Before we explore the Arigna tramway it is worth pausing for a moment to have a brief look at some of the C&L's rolling stock, both indigenous and imported.

Top left: **This is the classic C&L coach complete with a clerestory roof and balconies at either end. Coach No.9 was an all-third. Seen here at Ballinamore in 1932, it was scrapped in 1943.** H.C.Casserley.

Top right: **By the early 1950s many of the original carriages had been scrapped or were in a very run down condition. To help alleviate the situation, a former Tralee & Dingle coach, which had been running on the West Clare line, was sent to the C&L by CIE in 1954. No.21L had been repainted and had just arrived at Ballinamore when seen here in August 1954. The vehicle was**

built in 1907 by the Bristol Carriage and Wagon Company. D.G.Coakham.

Centre left: **No.17L was one of the original C&L 4-wheel brake vans. They had a balcony at one end only, but there was a door at the other enabling the guard to pass through the train from either end of his brake van. The 1950s CIE logo seen on this vehicle was colloquially known to railway enthusiasts as, 'the flying snail'.** H.C.Casserley.

Centre right: **No.7L began life looking like No.9 but was rebuilt at Inchicore in the early 1950s with a bus type body. In this guise it looked very like the railcar trailers supplied to the West Clare at around the same time.** John Edgington.

Bottom left: **At the same time as coach 21L arrived, another T&D vehicle, as it happens coupled to No.21L in this 1957 view, appeared on the C&L. Bogie van No.22L had begun life in 1890 as a brake third but was rebuilt as a van in 1940. Passenger services had been withdrawn on the T&D the previous year. Like the passenger coach, this vehicle was a product of the Bristol Carriage and Wagon Company.** D.G.Coakham.

Bottom right: **No.141L was one of a series of 4-wheeled wagons supplied by Pickerings in 1904 and 1912.** H.C.Casserley

Above: **Starting appropriately from the bay platform at Ballinamore, we will now venture down the tramway to Arigna and beyond up to the mines. By the end of the 1950s this was the last roadside tramway in the British Isles in regular service and with the periodic upsurges of coal traffic, at times it could be very busy indeed. On 1st July 1950, the C&L 4-4-0T No.3 waits in the bay with the 1.45pm to Arigna.** John Edgington.

Right: **The apparent double track stretch of line south of Ballinamore station was in fact worked as two separate single lines. The one on the left of the picture, along which the ex-T&D No.3 is heading, is for Arigna, that to the right is the C&L main line from Belturbet to Dromod.** Len's of Sutton.

Below: **The two lines soon went their separate ways. As No.3 heads for Arigna on 17th August 1957, the line to Dromod can be seen on the embankment behind the train.** D.G.Coakham.

Left, and below: **These pictures convey the very essence of the roadside tramway, the track undulates with the road which is empty of cars.** John Edgington.

Centre: **No.6T which was in charge of the 3.45pm to Arigna, on 26th May 1958, the day these pictures were taken, negotiates one of the number of ungated level crossings on the tramway. This one was near Drumshambo.** John Edgington.

Above and left: **Accidents at these crossings were not unheard of. On 8th June 1953, C&L 4-4-0T No.3 was hauling a train to Arigna which included a party of members of the Light Railway Transport League. As the train and a car approached the ungated level crossing at Mahanagh it appears that the cable which operated the car's brakes snapped with the consequences illustrated here. Despite being pushed a considerable distance by the train, the two occupants of the car were understandably shaken but thankfully, not badly hurt.** Both J.H.Price.

Top right: **In some places the tramway forsook the roadside and had its own right of way, as was the case at this point near Kiltubrid.** John Edgington.

Centre right: **This was the modest station of Kiltubrid, 9 miles from Ballinamore.** John Edgington.

Below: **Beyond Drumshambo the railway crossed over the upper reaches of Ireland's longest river, the *Shannon,* which was a relatively modest affair at this early stage of its journey to the sea. T&D No.3 heads a train for Ballinamore on 17th August 1957.** D.G.Coakham.

Bottom: **Drumshambo, at the head of Lough Allen, was the only village of any size on the tramway. T&D No.3 takes water there on 19th April 1955.** H.C.Casserley.

Top left: **Passenger trains never ventured further than Arigna station. No.3 has just arrived with the 1.55pm from Ballinamore on 19th April 1955.** H.C.Casserley.

Centre left: **The coal wagons in the distance will probably be added before No.6T works the 3.45pm departure back to Ballinamore on 26th May 1958.** John Edgington.

Centre right: **T&D No.3 takes empty wagons onto the branch leading up to the mines. The passenger station is in the distance.** Len's of Sutton.

Bottom: **The T&D No.3 again, this time on the extension proper, bringing a train of loaded coal wagons down from the mines and over the level crossing near Arigna station, on 28th July 1956.** D.G.Coakham.

Top: **Pictures of the loading facilities at the end of the tramway's 1920 extension seem to have been rarely published, which is surprising for Arigna's coal was the real reason that the C&L lasted so long. The coal was mined high up on the ridge behind No.8 and brought down to the terminus of the railway by a ropeway. Here it was processed and then loaded onto the narrow gauge wagons by means of the conveyor belt to the left of the loco.** D.G.Coakham.

Centre left: **No.6 positions empty wagons onto the siding leading to the loading point.** John Edgington.

Centre right: **It all looks a bit of a mess but it worked. No.8 pushes its train of wagons up to the loading point in May 1956.** D.G.Coakham.

Right: **On 26th May 1958 No.6T brings a loaded coal train down from the mines** John Edgington.

Appendix A

THE NARROW GAUGE IN INDUSTRY

I N MANY parts of the world substandard gauge railways are commonly found in industrial settings. Mines, quarries and large industrial sites often have their own narrow gauge railway systems. Despite Ireland's lack of a heavy industrial base a number of fascinating narrow gauge systems were operated at various times in different parts of the country. There is only room here to include a few of these systems but the ones I have chosen represent a very mixed bag indeed. I am indebted to the historian of these minor lines, Walter McGrath, for his generous assistance in the compilation of this part of the book.

THE ADMIRALTY RAILWAY
Haulbowline, County Cork

Large military establishments and their associated railways were not uncommon in Britain but rare in Ireland. In the nineteenth century the Admiralty developed a substantial naval base on Haulbowline Island in Cork Harbour. The main construction work began in 1865 and and continued for a further twenty two years. In the course of building the large dry dock and other facilities, a 3ft 6in gauge railway was constructed. About 3 miles of track were in use and two locos worked on it. From 1922 Haulbowline was taken over by the naval service of the Irish Free State. As late as the 1950s parts of the railway were still in use.

Above and below: **The mobile crane was still active as was the wagon which was used to dispose of rubbish. When full, in a fashion that would be frowned on today, its contents would be dumped into the harbour.** Both Walter McGrath collection.

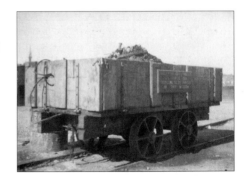

IRISH INDUSTRIAL MINERALS
Achill Island, County Mayo

Right: **From around 1910 to 1916 this
company operated a 2ft gauge line from its
quarry to the harbour at Keel on Achill
Island. A substance called whitestone was
quarried. This was used in the manufacture
of certain types of pottery. The whitestone
was shipped across Clew Bay to Westport
where it was milled. One of the locos used
on the line, an Orenstein and Koppel
0-4-0T built in Berlin and carrying the
name *Derwent*, is seen outside its shed on
Achill around 1912.**
Walter McGrath collection.

THE SHANNON ELECTRICITY SCHEME

Bottom right: **Between 1925 and 1930, the
biggest civil engineering project ever seen
in Ireland, was carried out by German
firms on behalf of the Irish government.
The works were designed to harness the
flow of the Shannon, the longest river in
the British Isles, to produce hydro-electric
power for the new Irish Free State, from a
generating station constructed at
Ardnacrusha. The contractors brought with
them an entire and substantial narrow
gauge railway system. At the height of the
work over 100 locos and 3,000 wagons
were operating on many miles of track. A
main line was constructed over 8 miles in
length from near the docks in Limerick,
through which plant was imported, to
O'Briensbridge in County Clare. Various
branches of this served the construction
sites along the way. In addition to this
system, which had a gauge of 900mm, a
web of light 600mm tracks was laid and
relocated as the work progressed. When
construction was completed the whole
railway was dismantled and shipped back
to Germany. Remarkably, by 1931 there
was scarcely a trace left of it. The sheer
scale of the Shannon scheme captured the
imagination of many people in Ireland and
led to a number of commercially printed
postcards of the works being made, and it
is one of these which is reproduced here.**
Des McGlynn collection.

THE GIANT EXCAVATOR & EMBANKMENT BUILDING MACHINES.
SHANNON ELECTRICITY SCHEME

THE MARCONI RAILWAY

Top: **In 1906 the pioneer of wireless, Guglielmo Marconi, chose a bleak and remote spot near Clifden in County Galway on the west coast of Ireland, as the site for a station to transmit radio messages across the Atlantic. The nearest road was 1¼ miles away from the selected site across boggy and marshy ground, and the only sensible way of transporting staff and equipment there was deemed to be by means of a narrow gauge railway. A 2ft gauge line was built. At first it was used to carry construction materials. Later, when the station was built, the railway transported turf and coal to feed the boilers which were used to generate the electricity that the transmitters required. A 0-4-0 saddle tank, built by Dick Kerr was used on the line and carried the wording, 'Marconi's Wireless Telegraph Company Ltd', on its tank.** Walter McGrath collection.

Centre left: **Fuel is being unloaded at the wireless station. The hoppers could be replaced with benches to convey workers to and from the site.**
Walter McGrath collection.

Left: **On 15th June 1919, John Alcock and Arthur Whitten Brown achieved immortality when they crash landed their Vickers Vimy aircraft near the Marconi station at Clifden, having become the first men to have flown the Atlantic non stop. They were entertained at the station, which flashed news of their flight to the world. They began their journey back to civilisation on this improvised railcar, believed to have been built at the Marconi factory in Chelmsford. The grim countenances of Alcock (left) and Whitten Brown may reflect the stress of the flight they have just made or apprehension at the prospect of bouncing across the bog on the railcar. This was the Marconi Railway's great moment of glory. It was closed down in 1922 when republicans burnt down the wireless station which was subsequently relocated to Wales.**
Walter McGrath collection.

THE GUINNESS BREWERY RAILWAY

Below: **Probably the best known industrial railway system in Ireland was that operated at the St James's Gate Brewery in Dublin by Guinness. There was an extensive network of 1ft 10in lines at different levels in the brewery on which ran a fleet of locos similar to No.17 depicted here. A special feature of the system was that the narrow gauge locos could be inserted by a crane into special broad gauge wagons, which were fitted with gears and rollers, transmitting the motion generated by the narrow gauge loco to the wheels of its broad gauge host, thus enabling the narrow gauge engine to shunt broad gauge wagons.** R.M.Casserley.

THE BORD NA MONA LINES

There are probably as many miles of 3ft gauge track in use today in Ireland as there was at the time of the First World War and this despite the closure of all the lines which make up the main part of this book. The answer to this apparent paradox is of course to be found in the large network of lines operated by Bord na Mona, the Irish Turf Board. It is impossible to give a precise figure as to the extent of the system as tracks are lifted and relaid all the time. There is only space here to have a glimpse of the system or rather systems, as there are separate self contained networks in various parts of the Irish Republic. The peat produced is either burned in special power stations or milled and packed for horticultural purposes. Our pictures come from various parts of Ireland over the last four decades.

Bottom: **In 1949 three 0-4-0 well tanks were supplied by Barclays of Kilmarnock to Bord na Mona. They had large fireboxes designed to burn turf. The native fuel did not suit them and they were quickly converted to burn coal. Though they were soon displaced by dieselisation, all three have happily been preserved. No.1 seen here at Portarlington in 1964, is now on the Shane's Castle Railway in County Antrim.** John Edgington.

Left: **On 12th June 1953 No.3 hauls a train of loaded bogie turf wagons on the Bord na Mona railway at Clonast. This loco was eventually bought by the Talyllyn Railway in Wales and has recently been radically rebuilt and regauged to become that line's No.7 *Tom Rolt*.** J.H.Price.

Below: **A 4-wheeled Rushton poses in front of the turf fired generating station.** John Edgington.

Bottom left: **By the time John Edgington** visited the system at Portarlington in June 1964 the steam locos had been supplanted by Rushton diesels. One of these gets some attention en route to the power station with a loaded train of bogie wagons.

Bottom right: **The Bord na Mona lines are as busy today as ever. This picture, taken in the late 1980s at the reception sidings at the power station at Lanesborough in County Longford, shows a Hunslet diesel arriving with a train of fifteen loaded wagons.** Des McGlynn.

Appendix B

THE NARROW GAUGE REVIVED

WHEN THE West Clare closed in 1961 it was no longer possible to buy a ticket and travel on a narrow gauge train in Ireland. Whilst the extensive network of lines operated by Bord na Mona kept the 3ft gauge alive in the country these were of course freight only lines. However in recent years there has been something of a resurgence in interest in the narrow gauge, not in its original capacity as a public transportation system, but as an attraction for tourists and the general public. This brief photographic appendix shows the lines that are active in the area covered by this book.

Right: **The Irish Steam Preservation Society have, for many years been running ex Bord na Mona 0-4-0WT No.2 on a line built from scratch through the grounds of Strad- bally Hall, in the village of the same name in County Laois. The coach is built on an ex C&L underframe and the brakevan came via the Shane's Castle Railway in County Antrim (see *The Irish Narrow Gauge Volume 2: The Ulster Lines*), from a line operated by British Aluminium in Scotland. The big weekend at Stradbally is in August when Ireland's largest steam rally is held on the site. This, combined with the narrow gauge railway, makes for one of the best and most informal steam weekends in Europe.** Des McGlynn.

Below: **Bord na Mona have begun to realise in recent years that there is a great deal of interest in their activities among the general public. A visitor centre has been set up at their workings at Blackwater in County Offaly and this special train is used to conduct visitors around the extensive bog workings in the area.** Des McGlynn.

Part of the former Tralee & Dingle Railway which closed in 1953 has been reopened as an attraction for the many thousands of visitors who flock to Kerry each year.

Left: **The 1892 built Hunslet 2-6-2T No.5 has been repatriated from the USA (where it went for preservation on the closure of the C&L in 1959) and restored for use on the section of the line which has been rebuilt, that between Tralee and Blennerville. Whilst this may not recapture the excitement of the old T&D with its ferocious gradients, the revived line should be on the itinerary of any railway enthusiast visiting Ireland. Our picture shows one of the first occasions the line was used in 1992, when it played host to some of the contestants in the annual 'Rose of Tralee' competition.**

Below: **Visitors to the Bord na Mona's Clonmacnoise and West Offaly Railway no doubt appreciate the comfort of the specially built coach and the matching livery of its diesel locomotive but connoisseurs of the Irish narrow gauge will be more interested in the other passenger vehicle on this line, which is no less than the coach part of one of the 1950s built railcars, No.3386, which used to run on the West Clare Railway.** Richard Whitford.

SELECT BIBLIOGRAPHY

abc Irish Locomotives: 1949 Edition; Ian Allan.

Conflict and Conciliation in Ireland 1890-1910: Bew; Oxford university Press, 1987.

Encyclopaedia of Narrow Gauge Railways of Great Britain and Ireland: Middlemass; Patrick Stephens Limited, 1991.

In The Tracks of the West Clare Railway: Lenihan; Mercier Press, 1990.

Ireland and the Death of Kindness: Gailey; Cork University Press, 1987.

Irish Steam: Nock; David and Charles, 1982.

Light and Narrow Gauge Locomotives: 2nd Edition, Kidner; Oakwood Press, 1949.

Light Railway Handbooks No.4 - Narrow Gauge Railways of Ireland: 3rd Edition, Kidner; Oakwood Press, 1949.

Some Industrial Railways of Ireland: McGrath; Walter McGrath, 1959.

The Cavan & Leitrim Railway: Flanagan; David and Charles, 1966.

The Cork, Blackrock & Passage Railway: Newham; Oakwood Press, 1970.

The Cork & Muskerry Light Railway: Newham, revised by Stanley C. Jenkins; Oakwood Press, 1992.

The Irish Administration 1801-1914: McDowell; Routledge and Kegan Paul, 1964.

The Irish Narrow Gauge Railway: Prideaux; David and Charles, 1981.

The Listowel & Ballybunion Railway: Newham, 1989 Edition revised by Michael Foster; Oakwood Press.

The Making of Modern Ireland: Beckett; Faber, 1981.

The Narrow Gauge Railways of Ireland: Fayle; Greenlake, 1946.

The Schull & Skibbereen Tramway: Newham; Oakwood Press, 1964.

The Tralee & Dingle Railway: Rowlands; Bradford Barton, 1977.

Journals

Journal of the Irish Railway Record Society, various issues.

Journal of the Kerry Archaelogical and Historical Society 1978, No.11: The Dingle Train.

The Railway Magazine, various issues.

INDEX

Numbers in *italic* refer to illustrations. Only one illustration is given for each entry in the index though in many cases, several photographs of the same geographical location or locomotive are to be found in the book. For towns which appear in the title of a railway company, i.e. Schull, see the reference to the railway itself, under 'Railway Companies'.

THE END

This picture seemed a most appropriate way to conclude this volume. Taken by J.H.Price in June 1953, it portrays what was probably the last passenger train to run on the Tralee & Dingle Railway, which by this time was owned by CIE.

The 'special' conveyed members of the Irish Railway Record Society and the Light Railway Transport League.

In the whole expanse of landscape visible in the picture, there is only one house to be seen. What chance had the railway of paying its way in such an environment and how could the labour intensive steam locomotive compete with buses and lorries, once the roads had been brought up to a reasonable standard?

The T&D, like so many of Ireland's minor lines, could scarcely cover its operating costs, even in the days when the railways only competition was the horse and cart.

By this time the Irish narrow gauge had become an anachronism, albeit for the railway enthusiast, a gloriously romantic one.

To those of us accustomed to the noise and bustle of the late twentieth century, the decades when the Dingle train and its sisters throughout Ireland, reigned supreme, do not seem now in retrospect, to have been bad times in which to live.